easy as
pie pops

easy as
pie pops

small in size and huge on flavor and fun

Andrea Smetona

founder of Cakewalk
Desserts

PAGE
PAGE STREET
PUBLISHING CO.

PAGE STREET
PUBLISHING CO.

First published in 2013 by

Page Street Publishing Co.

27 Congress Street, Suite 103

Salem, MA 01970

www.pagestreetpublishing.com

Distributed by Macmillan; sales in Canada by The Canadian Manda Group; distribution in Canada by The Jaguar Book Group.

16 15 14 13   1 2 3 4 5

ISBN-13: 978-1-62414-022-8

ISBN-10: 1-62414-022-X

Library of Congress Control Number: 2013942365

Cover and book design by Page Street Publishing

Photography by Bill Bettencourt

Printed and bound in China

Page Street is proud to be a member of 1% for the Planet. Members donate one percent of their sales to one or more of the over 1,500 environmental and sustainability charities across the globe who participate in this program.

For my mother

contents

Introduction

Something good is always better when it is shared with others. That's why I hope you'll enjoy making my recipes and will want to share them again and again.

I realize that recently there are a lot of cookbooks for mini treats, and while these can range from over-the-top and calorie-dense desserts to dietetic or healthier alternatives, I like to think my pie pop, cake pop and mini cake recipes fall somewhere in between, nutrition-wise— and above and beyond the rest when it comes to the flavor, the presentation and the fun of baking!

I like to promote using organically-grown fruit, vegetables and herbs when baking, if you can swing it. That's not to say I condemn frozen (or nonorganic) foods; I use them when I'm in a bind, or when I simply can't find the alternative. Keep in mind, however, that most fruits and veggies simply taste better when fresh and in season. I'm also going to say that, yes, most of these recipes call for sugar, butter and flour . . . but this is how I grew up baking. Desserts can be enjoyed to the fullest, especially when you consider this portion-controlled approach to enjoying them in moderation. This was how I came to find the value and demand in baking mini desserts that were not only delicious but bite size and beautiful to display!

AN INTRODUCTION TO PIE POPS

PIE POP TOOLS & TECHNIQUES

My pie pops are certainly eye-catching but they do take some attention to detail, as far as the technique goes. They consist of a bottom and top crust, with the pie filling pressed and sealed inside, creating a "pocket pie" on a stick. The sweet and savory pops have solid top crusts, with other ingredients or glazes for garnishes. The possibilities for the pop shapes are nearly endless, but the technique is pretty much the same for any pie pop you want to bake. Remember, you don't *need* all of these tools, but they will make your job a little easier if you plan to make pie pops again and again. All of these items can be found at your local grocery store in the baking aisle, at your nearest home-goods store or even online.

TOOLS FOR THE PIE POP CRUSTS

20" (50 cm) rolling pin

3" (7.5 cm)-diameter round, star-shaped and heart-shaped cookie cutters

1 ½" (4 cm) Linzer or mini cookie cutters (for the peek-a-boos)

Food processor or dough cutter

Large and medium-size mixing bowls

Measuring spoons

Measuring cups

Liquid measuring cups

Rubber spatula

Plastic wrap

Parchment paper

Resealable plastic freezer bags

PIE POP CRUST TECHNIQUE

1. Pick a selected pie pop from any of our featured recipes. You'll need to start with making the pie crust pastry, as this is a step that can and *should* be done ahead of time. Our Homemade Pie Pop Crust recipe (page 13) makes two 9″ (23 cm)-diameter crusts, which will be enough to make one dozen pie pops total (including top and bottom crusts). If desired, you can substitute enough unbaked store-bought or another homemade piecrust dough to make two 9-inch (23 cm)-diameter crusts. If you are making more pops, please adjust your recipe as needed. **TIP: I suggest making all of your crusts a day ahead of time and keeping them cold until you are ready to cut them into individual pop crusts.**

2. Once you are ready to begin making your pie pops, roll out and flour each side of the crust pastry before stamping out enough 3-inch (7.5 cm) rounds, hearts, stars or other shapes to make one dozen double-crusted pie pops. **TIP: Start stamping with the edges of the crust and work clockwise and inward to maximize the number or rounds your crust will produce. Do not piece together leftover crusts to form another round, as this will yield a cracked or crumbly pie pop.**

3. Once you cut have a total of twenty-four rounds from your two pieces of crust pastry, you can divide them in half equally (you need the same amount for bottom and top crusts of the pie pops), stack them and set aside. If you are doing a fruit pie, you can also stamp out the peek-a-boo designs from the top crusts at this time, and stack and set them aside. **TIP: Before stamping each peek-a-boo, make a small imprint with the tip of your fingernail to mark the center of each top crust, making it easier to center the peek-a-boo cutter.**

Once all the crusts are prepared and stacked, wrap the stacks in strips of parchment paper and place them in a resealable plastic freezer bag. You can now refrigerate them until you are ready to use.

TIME-SAVING TIPS

The crusts are the most important part of the pie pop, in my opinion, but they do take some time to make. Follow these time-saving tips to ensure you'll actually have *fun* baking your pretty pie pops.

- As I already mentioned, I highly recommend making your crusts ahead of time, unless you have four or five hours to dedicate to making your pie pops from start to finish.
- If you are not able to make your crusts ahead of time, I suggest buying refrigerated pie dough from your grocery store. These come boxed as 9-inch (23 cm)-diameter rounds of unbaked dough, typically found near the butter and cookie dough in the refrigerated section. This is also a great option if you want to make sure each pop looks uniformly similar or don't have the supplies for homemade crusts. Follow the same steps for prepping the refrigerated dough as you would the homemade dough.

TOOLS FOR PIE POPS

Large (12 qt [11 L]) stockpot

Colander

Large mixing bowl

Wooden spatula(s)

Metal slotted spoon

Measuring spoons

Measuring cups

Liquid measuring cups

Airtight glass storage containers

8" (20 cm)-long cookie sticks

Large cookie sheets

2 basting brushes (I prefer silicone brushes)

Small and medium-size mixing bowls

2 sugar shakers (I prefer confectioners' sugar shakers)

Flour sifter

Metal spoons

Nonstick cooking spray

Clear Jel modified cornstarch

Cooling rack(s)

Metal spatula

Food processor or blender

PIE POP FILLINGS & ASSEMBLY

All of the fruit pies call for making the filling from fresh fruit (or frozen, if not in season). The recipes instruct to wash and blanch the fruit in ½ gallon (2 liters) of boiling water, so this is where having a large stockpot comes in handy. **TIP: If you don't have a stockpot, you can always divide the batch in half and use two large saucepans instead.**

Once the selected fruit, sweet or savory pie filling is made, you can use it immediately for the pie pops or let it cool and store it in an airtight container. **TIP: I prefer glass jars (straight-sided or hermetic) but you can use any airtight container or even a heavy-duty resealable plastic bag.**

For easy dispensing, I suggest blending your fruit filling in a food processor or blender to eliminate large chunks of fruit (which will cause lumps and bumps in your pie pops and make it difficult to do the peek-a-boos). **TIP: I prefer pouring the blended fruit filling into 12-ounce (355 ml) squeeze bottles so that I can easily dispense the filling onto the bottom crust of the pie pops. This is an extra step, but it will save you loads of time and it tends to be a lot less messy than dispensing the filling using a spoon. Most grocery stores carry squirt bottles in the baking aisle.**

For sweet pie fillings, it's best to just spoon them onto the bottom piecrust; these fillings are often too dense to dispense via squeeze bottle. **TIP: You can also make these fillings a day or two ahead of time, to save time on the day of baking.**

Many savory pies are assembled in layers, so it's best to make all these fillings fresh on the day of baking. **TIP: Be careful not to overfill these pops, as it can be easy to do when trying to add all the layers successfully. Try chopping or cutting up all the ingredients as small as you can to prevent this.**

To bake your pie pops, you can use any cookie sheets you have on hand, but I prefer the rimless insulated ones by AirBake, which come in all different sizes. The 14 x 16-inch (35 x 40 cm) AirBake pan will fit twelve pie pops at a time and the insulated bottom ensures that each pop will bake nice and evenly. They also don't have rims, so it's much easier to access the pops when prepping and after baking. **TIP: Out of all the tools, I highly suggest investing in quality cookie sheets. Buy at least two so you can prep pops on one sheet while others are baking. Your cookie sheets will make or break your pops . . . literally.**

Homemade Pie Pop Crust

As with any great pie, we start with the crust. I've tried a few different recipes and always keep coming back to this one because it makes a nice even crust without lumps or inconsistencies, which can be an eyesore for pie pops. It's a universal recipe that works for all my vastly differing pops and is hearty enough to keep them secured on the stick (another important quality for pie pops). For some of the sweeter pies, where you would normally find a graham cracker crust, this crust is a great base for adding a garnish to give it that special taste, without jeopardizing the stability of the pop. All around, this is a great one to use for any pie pop recipe you find in this book. Happy baking!

YIELD: FOUR 9-INCH (23 CM)-DIAMETER PIECRUSTS

5 C (630 g) unbleached all-purpose flour

2 tsp salt

4 tbsp (50 g) sugar

24 tbsp (340 g) cold unsalted butter, cut into small pieces

1 C (224 g) vegetable shortening, chilled and cut into small pieces

½ C (120 ml) cold water

½ C (120 ml) white vinegar, chilled

In a food processor, blend 3 cups (380 g) of the flour and the salt and sugar until combined, about two 1-second pulses. Add the cold butter and shortening and process just until the dough starts to collect in uneven clumps, 10 to 15 seconds (there should be no uncoated flour).

Scrape the bowl with a rubber spatula and redistribute the dough evenly around the processor blade. Add the remaining 2 cups (250 g) of flour and pulse until the mixture is evenly distributed around the bowl and the mass of dough has been broken up (typically four to six pulses).

Empty the mixture into a medium-size mixing bowl. Pour the cold water and vinegar over the mixture. With a rubber spatula, use a folding motion to mix the dough, pressing down on the dough until it is slightly tacky and sticks together.

Divide the dough into two equal balls and flatten each into a 5-inch (12 cm) circle. Wrap each in plastic wrap and refrigerate for 1 hour (or up to 48 hours).

Once your dough is thoroughly chilled, roll out the dough between two pieces of plastic wrap to prevent the dough from sticking to the counter (and your roller). This will also eliminate the need to add more flour. Using a tapered rolling pill will also help keep the roundness in each crust.

If your dough has gotten too warm or sticky, slide it into the freezer for 10 to 15 minutes until it firms up again.

1

Fresh & Fruity
Pie Pops

These were the first pie pops I included on my pastry menu, and for good reason. They are easy to make, easy to bake and so colorful, fun and eye-catching—not to mention yummy! They are familiar and fresh, exciting and crowd-pleasing. In fact, I can't think of anyone that doesn't like fruit pie, or at least have one that is preferred or enjoyed above all others. So, I wanted to include all the old favorites, plus a few new combinations to add a little something special to my repertoire. These portable pocket pies are especially popular for their signature "peek-a-boos" and have made my business famous nationwide since they were added to my shop. They are also the easiest of all my pies to make as "low-sugar" or "sugar-substituted" and are easy to make completely organic. Win-win, in my book!

The peek-a-boo crusts do take a little more care and patience when preparing, but the payoff is well worth it. You can use any of the designs for any of the fruit flavors interchangeably, or add different designs altogether. Some favorites that I do seasonally are: Christmas trees, fall leaves, snowflakes and jack-o'-lanterns! I also do numbers or letters/monograms for adding a custom touch to birthday parties, weddings and anniversary celebrations. A stroll through the baking section of your nearest craft store will give you loads of possibilities for getting creative with the crusts. The fruit pies are typically the only ones that I recommend doing "peek-a-boo" crusts for, simply because of the nature of their pie filling. Fruit pies tend to overflow less while baking than some of the sweet or savory pies.

Even if you decide on doing most of your fruit pie pops with solid crusts, adding a few with "peek-a-boos" for a touch of flair easily livens up your pastry bouquet!

Cherry Tart

I don't think any cookbook would be complete without including cherry pie. It's simple yet full of flavor, if executed in the right way. Cherry Tart is one of my most popular (and most famously featured) pie pops, and with good reason. I use sour cherries for that added tart punch, and the signature heart peek-a-boo crust is adorable, fun and easily versatile. Of course, you can use the heart peek-a-boo crust on any of the berry pie pops, but the red cherry heart just fits so beautifully. Bake them with love.

YIELD: 2 DOZEN PIE POPS

1 recipe Homemade Pie Pop Crust (page 13), or 4 unbaked store-bought or homemade 9″ (23 cm)-diameter piecrusts

CHERRY FILLING

3 ½ C (580 g) pitted fresh sour cherries

6 tbsp (88 ml) freshly squeezed lemon juice

1 C (192 g) granulated sugar

⅓ C + 1 tbsp (59 g) Clear Jel, or 10 tbsp (94 g) cornstarch

1 ⅓ C (316 ml) cold water or cherry juice

⅛ tsp ground cinnamon

¼ tsp almond extract

6 drops red food coloring (optional)

1 large egg white, beaten, for brushing

Coarse sugar, for garnish

Preheat the oven to 400°F (204°C). Grease and flour a large baking sheet.

To prepare the filling: Bring ½ gallon (2 L) of water to a boil. Meanwhile, wash the cherries under cold water in a colander, picking out any leaves or stems. Pit the cherries and place in cold water until just covered, with the 4 tablespoons (59 ml) of the lemon juice to prevent browning. Blanch the cherries by placing them in the boiling water and bringing it back to a boil for 2 minutes. Drain the cherries and keep them covered in a large bowl.

In a large pot, combine the granulated sugar, Clear Jel (or cornstarch), cold water (or cherry juice), cinnamon, almond extract and food coloring. Stir the mixture over medium heat until it thickens and begins to boil. Add the remaining 2 tablespoons (29 ml) of lemon juice and, stirring, continue to boil for 1 minute.

Remove from the heat and fold the berries into the hot mixture, stirring gently. Let cool to room temperature. Transfer the mixture to a food processor or blender and pulse for 4 to 5 seconds. Set aside.

To assemble the pie pops: Flour both sides of the two piecrusts, then roll flat with a rolling pin. Using a 3-inch (7.6 cm) round cookie cutter, cut twenty-four rounds from the dough, twelve for the bottom crust and twelve for the top crust. If doing peek-a-boo, stamp out a heart peek-a-boo from each of the twelve top crusts, using a heart-shaped Linzer cookie cutter.

Lay out the twelve bottom crusts on the prepared baking sheet. Brush each bottom crust with beaten egg white, using a silicone basting brush. Press an 8-inch (20 cm)-long cookie stick firmly on top of the center of each bottom crust.

(continued)

Dispense a 1 ½-inch (about 4 cm) dollop of cherry filling in the center of each bottom crust. Place a top crust over each bottom crust and press firmly around the sides only, sealing the filling inside.

Create a cookie stick dowel by cutting a 1-inch (2.5 cm)-long piece off the end of an 8-inch (20 cm) cookie stick. Use this dowel to crimp the sealed edges of the pie pop by pressing firmly on each side of the stick first, then move counterclockwise around the edges. This will keep the stick from moving around once the pie pop is baked.

After each pop is sealed and pressed, carefully brush more egg white on each top crust, except over the filling inside the peek-a-boo opening. Finally, sprinkle the top crusts with coarse sugar.

Bake the sheet on the center rack of the oven for 15 minutes, until the crust is nice and golden. Then place the individual pops on a cooling rack and let cool for at least 15 minutes before serving.

Caramel Apple

When the fair came into town, part of the whole experience was to buy a caramel apple and have it all over your face by the time you were finished. I wanted to duplicate this nostalgic treat in a pie pop with less mess to clean up afterward. You can always make homemade caramel, but I favor the ease of the prepackaged candy caramels. These little pops are great for any fall-themed party or celebration and are a great way to steer clear of the expected!

YIELD: 2 DOZEN PIE POPS

---

1 recipe Homemade Pie Pop Crust (page 13), or 4 unbaked store-bought or homemade 9" (23 cm)-diameter piecrusts

TAFFY
½ C (100 g) light brown sugar, packed

¼ C (57 g) butter, melted

⅓ C (33 g) all-purpose flour

CARAMEL APPLE FILLING
5 C (900 g) thinly sliced Granny Smith apples

⅔ C (128 g) granulated sugar

3 tbsp (18 g) all-purpose flour

2 tsp ground cinnamon

1 tsp freshly squeezed lemon juice

10 caramels, halved

2 tbsp (29 ml) milk

1 large egg white, beaten, for brushing

1:1 mixture of coarse sugar and ground cinnamon, for garnish

Preheat the oven to 350°F (176°C). Grease and flour a large baking sheet.

To prepare the taffy: In a small bowl, combine the brown sugar, melted butter and flour. Mix well and set aside.

To prepare the filling: Place the apples in a large bowl with the lemon juice and toss. Add the granulated sugar, flour, cinnamon and milk. Toss until all the ingredients are well mixed and the apples are thoroughly coated.

Spoon half of the apple filling into a 9-inch (23 cm)-diameter deep pie dish. Top with a layer of half of the caramels and then with a layer of half of the taffy mixture. Repeat the process with remaining apple mixture, caramels and taffy mixture.

Cover with foil and place in the oven with a baking sheet underneath to catch any overspills. Bake for 25 minutes. Remove the foil and bake for another 20 to 25 minutes. Remove from the oven and let cool to room temperature, then blend the entire pie filling in a food processor or blender until the apples are well blended. Increase oven temperature to 375°F (190°C).

To assemble the pie pops: Flour both sides of the two piecrusts, then roll flat with a rolling pin. Using a 3-inch (7.6 cm) round cookie cutter, cut twenty-four rounds from the dough, twelve for the bottom crust and twelve for the top crust. Using an apple-shaped Linzer cookie cutter, make twelve cutouts of dough from the scrap dough to garnish the top crusts.

Lay out the twelve bottom crusts on the prepared baking sheet. Brush each bottom crust with beaten egg white, using a silicone basting brush. Press an 8-inch (20 cm)-long cookie stick firmly on top of the center of each bottom crust.

(continued)

Dispense a 1 ½-inch (about 4 cm) dollop of caramel apple filling in the center of each bottom crust. Place a top crust over each bottom crust and press firmly around the sides only, sealing the filling inside.

Create a cookie stick dowel by cutting a 1-inch (2.5 cm)-long piece off the end of an 8-inch (20 cm)-long cookie stick. Use this dowel to crimp the sealed edges of the pie pop by pressing firmly on each side of the stick first, then move counterclockwise around the edges. This will keep the stick from moving around once the pie pop is baked.

After each pop is sealed and pressed, brush more egg white on each top crust. Center a mini apple cutout on each top crust, pressing it down and brushing it with egg white. Finally, sprinkle the top crusts with the cinnamon sugar.

Bake the sheet on the center rack of the oven for 15 to 18 minutes, until the crust is nice and golden. Then place the individual pops on a cooling rack and let cool for at least 15 minutes before serving.

Vintage Blackberry

When I think of a classic pie, I immediately think of the handmade woven lattice crust. This traditional and bold berry pie makes for a perfect centerpiece at any celebration and using a lattice mold makes the "woven" effect quick and foolproof! If you are not partial to seeds, you can strain them out, using a sieve or food mill; however, I always leave them in for that fresh-picked taste. Don't forget to garnish with coarse sugar on top for that added sparkle and finishing touch.

YIELD: 2 DOZEN PIE POPS

1 recipe Homemade Pie Pop Crust (page 13), or 4 unbaked store-bought or homemade 9" (23 cm)-diameter piecrusts

BLACKBERRY FILLING

5 C (497 g) fresh blackberries

½ C (96 g) granulated sugar

¼ C (38 g) Clear Jel, or 10 tbsp (94 g) cornstarch

1 C (236 ml) cold water

1 tbsp (14 ml) freshly squeezed lemon juice

1 large egg white, beaten, for brushing

Coarse sugar, for garnish

Preheat the oven to 400°F (204°C). Grease and flour a large baking sheet.

To prepare the filling: Bring ½ gallon (2 L) of water to a boil. Meanwhile, wash the blackberries under cold water in a colander, picking out any leaves or stems. Blanch them by placing them in the boiling water and bringing it back to a boil for 2 minutes. Drain the berries and keep them covered in a large bowl.

In a large pot, combine the granulated sugar, Clear Jel (or cornstarch) and cold water. Stir the mixture over medium heat until it thickens and begins to boil. Add the lemon juice and, stirring, continue to boil for 1 minute.

Remove from the heat and fold the berries into the hot mixture, stirring gently. Let cool to room temperature. Transfer the mixture to a food processor or blender and pulse for 4 to 5 seconds.

To assemble the pie pops: Flour both sides of the two piecrusts, then roll flat with a rolling pin. Using a 3-inch (7.6 cm) round cookie cutter, cut twenty-four rounds from the dough, twelve for the bottom crust and twelve for the top crust. If doing peek-a-boo, stamp out a lattice peek-a-boo from each of the twelve top crusts, using a lattice pie mold or press.

Lay out the twelve bottom crusts on the prepared baking sheet. Brush each bottom crust with egg white, using a silicone basting brush. Press an 8-inch (20 cm)-long cookie stick firmly on top of the center of each bottom crust.

Dispense a 1 ½-inch (about 4 cm) dollop of blackberry filling in the center of each bottom crust. Place the top crust over each bottom crust and press firmly around the sides only, sealing the filling inside.

(continued)

Create a cookie stick dowel by cutting a 1-inch (2.5 cm)-long piece off the end of an 8-inch (20 cm)-long cookie stick. Use this dowel to crimp the sealed edges of the pie pop by pressing firmly on each side of the stick first, then move counterclockwise around the edges. This will keep the stick from moving around once the pie pop is baked.

After each pop is sealed and pressed, carefully brush more egg white on each lattice top, except over the filling inside the openings. Finally, sprinkle the top crusts with coarse sugar.

Bake the sheet on the center rack of the oven for 15 minutes, until the crust is nice and golden. Then place the individual pops on a cooling rack and let cool for at least 15 minutes before serving.

fresh & fruity pie pops

Blueberry Bouquet

My grandmother always grew blueberries in her garden, and I remember she once tried shipping me a bushel of blueberries so I could enjoy them when we were unable to visit that summer. Unfortunately, they arrived mashed and spoiled, but I never had the heart to tell her that they didn't make it. Fortunately, I've found a great way to commemorate her in this beautiful blueberry pop featuring an adorable flower peek-a-boo! This pop is dedicated to you, Grandma Dorothy.

YIELD: 2 DOZEN PIE POPS

1 recipe Homemade Pie Pop Crust (page 13), or 4 unbaked store-bought or homemade 9" (23 cm)-diameter piecrusts

BLUEBERRY FILLING

4 C (397 g) fresh blueberries

¾ C (143 g) granulated sugar

⅓ C + 1 tbsp (59 g) Clear Jel, or 10 tbsp (94 g) cornstarch

1 C (236 ml) cold water and/or blueberry juice

3 ½ tsp (17 ml) freshly squeezed lemon juice

1 large egg white, beaten, for brushing

Coarse sugar, for garnish

Preheat the oven to 400°F (204°C). Grease and flour a large baking sheet.

To prepare the filling: Bring ½ gallon (2 L) of water to a boil. Meanwhile, wash the blueberries under cold water in a colander, picking out any leaves or stems. Blanch them by placing them in the boiling water and bringing it back to a boil for 2 minutes. Drain the berries and keep them covered in a large bowl.

In a large pot, combine the granulated sugar, Clear Jel (or cornstarch) and cold water (or blueberry juice). Stir the mixture over medium heat until it thickens and begins to boil. Add the lemon juice and, stirring, continue to boil for 1 minute.

Remove from the heat and fold the berries into the hot mixture, stirring gently. Let cool to room temperature. Transfer the mixture to a food processor or blender and pulse for 4 to 5 seconds.

To assemble the pie pops: Flour both sides of the two piecrusts, then roll flat with a rolling pin. Using a 3-inch (7.6 cm) round cookie cutter, cut twenty-four rounds from the dough, twelve for the bottom crust and twelve for the top crust. If doing peek-a-boo, stamp out a flower-shaped peek-a-boo from each of the twelve top crusts, using a flower-shaped Linzer cookie cutter.

Lay out the twelve bottom crusts on the prepared baking sheet. Brush each bottom crust with egg white, using a silicone basting brush. Press an 8-inch (20 cm)-long cookie stick firmly on top of the center of each bottom crust.

Dispense a 1 ½-inch (about 4 cm) dollop of blueberry filling in the center of each bottom crust. Place a top crust over each bottom crust and press firmly around the sides only, sealing the filling inside.

(continued)

Create a cookie stick dowel by cutting a 1-inch (2.5 cm)-long piece off the end of an 8-inch (20 cm)-long cookie stick. Use this dowel to crimp the sealed edges of the pie pop by pressing firmly on each side of the stick first, then move counterclockwise around the edges. This will keep the stick from moving around once the pie pop is baked.

After each pop is sealed and pressed, carefully brush more egg white on each top crust, except over the filling inside the peek-a-boo opening. Finally, sprinkle the top crusts with coarse sugar.

Bake the sheet on the center rack of the oven for 15 minutes, until the crust is nice and golden. Then place the individual pops on a cooling rack and let cool for at least 15 minutes before serving.

Strawberry Limeade

I remember going to the local Sonic Drive-In as a teen and getting a *big* strawberry limeade drink during those hot Texas summers (and winters, as a matter of fact). The flavors are actually very complelmentary with the sweet and sour, and are just as tasty served warm. I love to display these pie pops in a clear vase filled with small limes, for a beautiful pop of green. They're also perfect for barbecues and are super easy to bring along for picnics!

YIELD: 2 DOZEN PIE POPS

1 recipe Homemade Pie Pop Crust (page 13), or 4 unbaked store-bought or homemade 9″ (23 cm)-diameter piecrusts

STRAWBERRY & LIME FILLING

3 ½ C (33 g) strawberries, hulled and sliced

¾ C (143 g) granulated sugar

¼ C + 1 tbsp (122 g) Clear Jel, or 10 tbsp (94 g) cornstarch

1 C (236 ml) cold water

3 ½ tbsp (51 ml) freshly squeezed lemon juice

1 tbsp (9 g) lime zest

¼ C (59 ml) freshly squeezed lime juice

1 large egg white, beaten, for brushing

Coarse sugar, for garnish

Preheat the oven to 400°F (204°C). Grease and flour a large baking sheet.

To prepare the filling: Bring ½ gallon (2 L) of water to a boil. Meanwhile, wash the strawberries under cold water in a colander, picking out any leaves or stems. Blanch them by placing them in the boiling water and bringing it back to a boil for 2 minutes. Drain the berries and keep them covered in a large bowl.

In a large pot, combine the granulated sugar, Clear Jel (or cornstarch) and pcold water. Stir the mixture over medium heat until it thickens and begins to boil. Add the lemon juice and, stirring, continue to boil for 1 minute.

Remove from the heat and fold the berries, lime zest and lime juice into the hot mixture, stirring gently. Let cool to room temperature. Transfer the mixture to a food processor or blender and pulse for 4 to 5 seconds.

To assemble the pie pops: Flour both sides of the two piecrusts, then roll flat with a rolling pin. Using a 3-inch (7.6 cm) round cookie cutter, cut twenty-four rounds from the dough, twelve for the bottom crust and twelve for the top crust. If doing peek-a-boo, stamp out a star-shaped peek-a-boo from each of the twelve top crusts, using a star-shaped Linzer cookie cutter.

Lay out the twelve bottom crusts on the prepared baking sheet. Brush each bottom crust with egg white, using a silicone basting brush. Press an 8-inch (20 cm)-long cookie stick firmly on top of the center of each bottom crust.

Dispense a 1 ½-inch (about 4 cm) dollop of strawberry limeade filling in the center of each bottom crust. Place a top crust over each bottom crust and press firmly around the sides only, sealing the filling inside.

(continued)

Create a cookie stick dowel by cutting a 1-inch (2.5 cm)-long piece off the end of an 8-inch (20 cm)-long cookie stick. Use this dowel to crimp the sealed edges of the pie pop by pressing firmly on each side of the stick first, then move counterclockwise around the edges. This will keep the stick from moving around once the pie pop is baked.

After each pop is sealed and pressed, carefully brush more egg white on each top crust, except over the filling inside the peek-a-boo opening. Finally, sprinkle the top crusts with coarse sugar.

Bake the sheet on the center rack of the oven for 15 minutes, until the crust is nice and golden. Then place the individual pops on a cooling rack and let cool for at least 15 minutes before serving.

D'Anjou Pear

In this recipe, the subtly sweet pear balances the richness of the white chocolate and makes for a visually splendid surprise! There's something cozy and inviting about these pops, which makes them good for large gatherings but also perfect for enjoying alone with a hot cup of coffee and a good book.

YIELD: 2 DOZEN PIE POPS

1 recipe Homemade Pie Pop Crust (page 13), or 4 unbaked store-bought or homemade 9" (23 cm)-diameter piecrusts

PEAR FILLING

½ C (95 g) granulated sugar

3 tbsp (18 g) all-purpose flour

¼ tsp salt

1 tsp ground cinnamon

¼ tsp ground nutmeg

1 tsp lemon zest

1 tbsp (14 g) butter, at room temperature

5 C (899 g) cored and chopped D'Anjou Pears (skin on)

½ C (90 g) white chocolate chips

1 tbsp (14 ml) freshly squeezed lemon juice

1 large egg white, beaten, for brushing

1:1 mixture of coarse sugar and ground cinnamon

Preheat the oven to 450°F (232°C). Grease and flour a large baking sheet.

To prepare the filling: Combine the granulated sugar, flour, salt, cinnamon, nutmeg and lemon zest in a large mixing bowl; cut in the butter until the mixture resembles coarse crumbs.

In another bowl, mix together the pears, chocolate chips and lemon juice. In a 9-inch (23 cm) pie dish, alternate between pear and sugar mixtures. Bake at 450°F (232°C) for 10 minutes then reduce temperature to 350°F (176°C) and bake for an additional 35-35 minutes or until set. Use filling immediately. Increase oven temperature to 375°F (190°C).

To assemble the pie pops: Flour both sides of the two piecrusts, then roll flat with a rolling pin. Using a 3-inch (7.6 cm) round cookie cutter, cut twenty-four rounds from the dough, twelve for the bottom crust and twelve for the top crust.

Lay out the twelve bottom crusts on the prepared baking sheet. Brush each bottom crust with egg white, using a silicone basting brush. Press an 8-inch (20 cm)-long cookie stick firmly on top of the center of each bottom crust.

Dispense a 1 ½-inch (about 4 cm) dollop of pear filling in the center of each bottom crust. Place a top crust over each bottom crust and press firmly around the sides only, sealing the filling inside.

Create a cookie stick dowel by cutting a 1-inch (2.5 cm)-long piece off the end of an 8-inch (20 cm)-long cookie stick. Use this dowel to crimp the sealed edges of the pie pop by pressing firmly on each side of the stick first, then move counterclockwise around the edges.

After each pop is sealed and pressed, brush more egg white on each top crust. Finally, sprinkle the top crusts with the cinnamon sugar.

Bake the sheet on the center rack of the oven for 15 to 18 minutes, until the crust is nice and golden. Then place the individual pops on a cooling rack and let cool for at least 15 minutes before serving.

Old-Fashioned Apple

This pie is part of American history! It's been a favorite since the birth of our country, and is still an icon today. This is a great one to include in your baking repertoire, for those looking for a familiar or well-loved flavor. They're as American as, well, apple pie.

YIELD: 2 DOZEN PIE POPS

1 recipe Homemade Pie Pop Crust (page 13), or 4 unbaked store-bought or homemade 9" (23 cm)-diameter piecrusts

APPLE FILLING

6 to 8 medium-size Fuji, McIntosh, Jonathan, and/or Gala apples

1 C (191 g) granulated sugar

½ tsp ground cinnamon

¼ tsp ground nutmeg

¼ tsp ground cloves

¼ tsp ground ginger

¼ tsp ground allspice

¾ C (177 ml) 100% apple juice

½ C (118 ml) cold water

2 tbsp (29 ml) freshly squeezed lemon juice

5 tbsp (47 g) Clear Jel, or 5 tbsp (47 g) cornstarch

1 large egg white, beaten, for brushing

1:1 mixture of coarse sugar and ground cinnamon, for garnish

Preheat the oven to 400°F (204°C). Grease and flour a large baking sheet.

To prepare the filling: Bring ½ gallon (2 L) of water to a boil. Meanwhile, wash the whole apples under warm water, then peel, core and slice them into ¼- to ½-inch (0.6 to 1.27 cm) slices until you get 3 ½ cups (629 g) of sliced apple. Blanch the apple slices by placing them in the boiling water and bringing it back to a boil for 2 minutes. Drain the apples and keep them covered in a large bowl.

In a large pot, combine the granulated sugar, spices, apple juice and cold water. Stir the mixture over medium-high heat until it thickens and begins to bubble. In a mixing bowl, mix the lemon juice with the Clear Jel (or cornstarch) and add to the boiling mixture. Continue stirring until the mixture is thick but still flows.

Remove from the heat and fold the apple slices into the hot mixture, stirring gently. Let cool to room temperature. Transfer the mixture to a food processor or blender and pulse for 5 to 10 seconds, until there are no large apple chunks.

To assemble the pie pops: Flour both sides of the two piecrusts, then roll flat with a rolling pin. Using a 3-inch (7.6 cm) round cookie cutter, cut twenty-four rounds from the dough, twelve for the bottom crust and twelve for the top crust. If doing peek-a-boo, stamp out an apple-shaped peek-a-boo from each of the twelve top crusts, using an apple-shaped Linzer cookie cutter.

Lay out the twelve bottom crusts on the prepared baking sheet. Brush each bottom crust with egg white, using a silicone basting brush. Press an 8-inch (20 cm)-long cookie stick firmly on top of the center of each bottom crust.

Dispense a 1 ½-inch (about 4 cm) dollop of apple filling in the center of each bottom crust. Place a top crust over each bottom crust and press firmly around the sides only, sealing the filling inside.

(continued)

Create a cookie stick dowel by cutting a 1-inch (2.5 cm)-long piece off the end of an 8-inch (20 cm)-long cookie stick. Use this dowel to crimp the sealed edges of the pie pop by pressing firmly on each side of the stick first, then move counterclockwise around the edges. This will keep the stick from moving around once the pie pop is baked.

After each pop is sealed and pressed, carefully brush more egg white on each top crust, except over the filling inside the peek-a-boo opening. Finally, sprinkle the top crusts with the cinnamon sugar.

Bake the sheet on the center rack of the oven for 15 minutes, until the crust is nice and golden. Then place the individual pops on a cooling rack and let cool for at least 15 minutes before serving.

Peachy Keen

Peaches are a favorite stone fruit of mine, and because they are super juicy and sweet, they make for some mighty fine pies. This fruit pie works well with one of my peek-a-boo designs as well (the lattice and the heart are always popular), but you can really seal in the freshness of the fresh peaches by making the top crust solid and simply glazing it for that added sweet touch. Peach pie pops . . . soon to be a summer must-have!

YIELD: 2 DOZEN PIE POPS

---

1 recipe Homemade Pie Pop Crust (page 13), or 4 unbaked store-bought or homemade 9" (23 cm)-diameter piecrusts

PEACH FILLING

7 medium fresh peaches

¼ C (59 ml) freshly squeezed lemon juice, plus more for coating peach slices

¼ C + 1 tbsp (47 g) Clear Jel, or 10 tbsp (94 g) cornstarch

¾ C (177 ml) cold water

1 C (191 g) granulated sugar

⅛ tsp ground cinnamon

⅛ tsp almond extract

VANILLA GLAZE

1 tsp butter

1 ½ C (195 g) confectioners' sugar

2 tbsp (29 ml) milk or water

¼ tsp vanilla extract

1 large egg white, beaten, for brushing

Preheat the oven to 375°F (190°C). Grease and flour a large baking sheet.

To prepare the filling: Bring a large pot of water to a boil, and have ready a bowl of ice water. Meanwhile, wash the peaches in a colander under cold water. Peel by placing peaches in the boiling water for 30 to 60 seconds, then placing them in ice water (the skins will come off easily). Slice or cut into chunks (you should have about 3 ½ cups [629 g]), removing the pits and any bruised flesh. Place the peach slices in a large bowl and coat with lemon juice making sure to keep ¼ cup (59 ml) aside.

In a large pot, combine the Clear Jel (or cornstarch), cold water, granulated sugar, cinnamon and almond extract. Stir the mixture over medium-high heat until it thickens and begins to boil. Add the ¼ cup (59 ml) of lemon juice and continue to boil for 1 minute, stirring constantly.

Add the peaches to the mixture and continue to heat for 3 more minutes. Remove from the heat and let cool to room temperature. Transfer the mixture to a food processor or blender and pulse for 4 to 5 seconds.

To prepare the glaze: Melt the butter in a small pan, then add all the other ingredients. Stir until creamy. If the glaze is too runny, add more sugar; if it is too thick, add more water ½ teaspoon at a time.

To assemble the pie pops: Flour both sides of the two piecrusts, then roll flat with a rolling pin. Using a 3-inch (7.6 cm) round cookie cutter, cut twenty-four rounds from the dough, twelve for the bottom crust and twelve for the top crust.

Lay out the twelve bottom crusts on the prepared baking sheet. Brush each bottom crust with egg white, using a silicone basting brush. Press an 8-inch (20 cm)-long cookie stick firmly on top of the center of each bottom crust.

(continued)

Dispense a 1 ½-inch (about 4 cm) dollop of peach filling in the center of each bottom crust. Place a top crust over each bottom crust and press firmly around the sides only, sealing the filling inside.

Create a cookie stick dowel by cutting a 1-inch (2.5 cm)-long piece off the end of an 8-inch (20 cm)-long cookie stick. Use this dowel to crimp the sealed edges of the pie pop by pressing firmly on each side of the stick first, then move counterclockwise around the edges. This will keep the stick from moving around once the pie pop is baked.

After each pop is sealed and pressed, brush more egg white on each top crust.

Bake the sheet on the center rack of the oven for 15 to 18 minutes, until the crust is nice and golden. Then place the individual pops on a cooling rack. While the pops are still warm, brush the glaze over the top of each crust. Allow to dry completely before handling and let cool for at least 15 minutes before serving.

Strawberry Rhubarb

It takes a little bit of skill to successfully combine fruit and vegetables into one dish, let alone a dessert, but my Strawberry Rhubarb pie pop does just that. The tart and bitter rhubarb and the sweet strawberries marry beautifully as they bake together. Their rich colors break down to add a delightfully pastel pink color to the pastry. It's the original odd couple, but oh so good!

YIELD: 2 DOZEN PIE POPS

---

1 recipe Homemade Pie Pop Crust (page 13), or 4 unbaked store-bought or homemade 9″ (23 cm)-diameter piecrusts

STRAWBERRY & RHUBARB FILLING

3 C (454 g) strawberries, hulled and sliced

3 C (688 g) rhubarb stalks, cut into 1″ (2.5 cm) pieces

1 tbsp (9 g) orange zest

¾ C (143 g) granulated sugar

2 tsp freshly squeezed lemon juice

¼ tsp vanilla extract

¼ C (52 g) instant tapioca

2 tbsp (28 g) butter, cut into small pieces

PINK VANILLA GLAZE

1 tsp butter

1 ½ C (12 g) confectioners' sugar

2 tbsp (29 ml) milk or water

¼ tsp vanilla extract

1 drop pastel pink food coloring, or ½ drop of red

1 large egg white, beaten, for brushing

Preheat the oven to 350°F (176°C). Grease and flour a large baking sheet.

To prepare the filling: Combine the strawberries, rhubarb, orange zest, granulated sugar, lemon juice, vanilla, tapioca and butter in a large bowl.

Pour into a 9-inch (23 cm)-diameter pie dish and bake for 15 to 20 minutes to soften. Remove from the oven and let cool to room temperature. Transfer the mixture to a food processor or blender and pulse for 4 to 5 seconds. Increase the oven temperature to 375°F (190°C).

To prepare the glaze: Melt the butter in a small pan, then add all the other ingredients. Stir until creamy. If the glaze is too runny, add more sugar; if it is too thick, add more water ½ teaspoon at a time.

To assemble the pie pops: Flour both sides of the two piecrusts, then roll flat with a rolling pin. Using a 3-inch (7.6 cm) round cookie cutter, cut twenty-four rounds from the dough, twelve for the bottom crust and twelve for the top crust.

Lay out the twelve bottom crusts on the prepared baking sheet. Brush each bottom crust with egg white, using a silicone basting brush. Press an 8-inch (20 cm)-long cookie stick firmly on top of the center of each bottom crust.

Dispense a 1 ½-inch (about 4 cm) dollop of strawberry filling in the center of each bottom crust. Place a top crust over each bottom crust and press firmly around the sides only, sealing the filling inside.

(continued)

Create a cookie stick dowel by cutting a 1-inch (2.5 cm)-long piece off the end of an 8-inch (20 cm)-long cookie stick. Use this dowel to crimp the sealed edges of the pie pop by pressing firmly on each side of the stick first, then move counterclockwise around the edges. This will keep the stick from moving around once the pie pop is baked.

After each pop is sealed and pressed, brush more egg white on each top crust.

Bake the sheet on the center rack of the oven for 15 to 18 minutes, until the crust is nice and golden. Then place the individual pops on a cooling rack. While the pops are still warm, brush the glaze over the top of each crust. Allow to dry completely before handling and let cool for at least 15 minutes before serving.

Cranberry-Walnut Crisp

Adding tart cranberries to cinnamon-spiced apples definitely reminds me of the holidays, but these flavor profiles are popular enough to be enjoyed year-round as well. I've had people who don't even care for cranberries crave these delectable pops.

YIELD: 2 DOZEN PIE POPS

1 recipe Homemade Pie Pop Crust (page 13), or 4 unbaked store-bought or homemade 9" (23 cm)-diameter piecrusts

CRANBERRY-WALNUT FILLING

2 C (12 g) fresh or frozen cranberries

1 C (116 g) chopped walnuts

¼ C (201 g) brown sugar

1 large egg

½ C (95 g) granulated sugar

⅓ C (76 g) butter, melted and cooled

½ C (49 g) all-purpose flour

CRISP TOPPING

1 C (201 g) brown sugar

¾ C (74 g) all-purpose flour

¾ C (80 g) old-fashioned or quick rolled oats (not instant)

½ tsp ground cinnamon

¼ tsp salt

½ C (114 g) cold butter

1 large egg white, beaten, for brushing

Preheat the oven to 325°F (162°C). Grease a 9-inch (23 cm)-diameter pie dish, and grease and flour a large baking sheet.

To prepare the filling: Wash and drain the cranberries. In a large bowl, mix together the cranberries, walnuts and brown sugar. Spread in the prepared pie dish and pat down.

In another bowl, combine the egg, granulated sugar, melted butter and flour; beat well. Spread the egg mixture on top of the mixture in the pie dish.

Bake for 40 to 45 minutes. Remove from the oven and let cool to room temperature. Increase the oven temperature to 375°F (190°C).

To prepare the topping: In a large mixing bowl, combine all the topping ingredients, except the butter. Using a pastry blender or a fork, cut the butter into the mixture until it resembles coarse bread crumbs.

To assemble the pie pops: Flour both sides of the two piecrusts, then roll flat with a rolling pin. Using a 3-inch (7.6 cm) round cookie cutter, cut twenty-four rounds from the dough, twelve for the bottom crust and twelve for the top crust.

Lay out the twelve bottom crusts on the prepared baking sheet. Brush each bottom crust with egg white, using a silicone basting brush. Press an 8-inch (20 cm)-long cookie stick firmly on top of the center of each bottom crust.

Dispense a 1 ½-inch (about 4 cm) dollop of cranberry filling in the center of each bottom crust. Place a top crust over each bottom crust and press firmly around the sides only, sealing the filling inside.

(continued)

Create a cookie stick dowel by cutting a 1-inch (2.5 cm)-long piece off the end of an 8-inch (20 cm)-long cookie stick. Use this dowel to crimp the sealed edges of the pie pop by pressing firmly on each side of the stick first, then move counterclockwise around the edges. This will keep the stick from moving around once the pie pop is baked.

After each pop is sealed and pressed, brush more egg white on each top crust. Finally, sprinkle the top crusts with the crisp topping.

Bake the sheet on the center rack of the oven for 15 to 18 minutes, until the crust is nice and golden. Then place the individual pops on a cooling rack. Allow to dry completely before handling and let cool for at least 15 minutes before serving.

Blueberry-Pomegranate

My two favorite superfoods are blueberries and pomegranates. Put them together in a pie, and you have a scrumptious little pastry that is rich in vitamins and antioxidants and also big on flavor. Pomegranate seeds have such a juicy sharpness to them, I often find myself eating them with creamy yogurt or granola to subdue them just a bit . . . but not too much. That's why blueberries make a wonderful pairing with pomegranate. The combination is subtle, sweet and a little unexpected.

YIELD: 2 DOZEN PIE POPS

1 recipe Homemade Pie Pop Crust (page 13), or 4 unbaked store-bought or homemade 9" (23 cm)-diameter piecrusts

BLUEBERRY-POMEGRANATE FILLING

3 C (298 g) fresh blueberries

½ C (80 g) pomegranate seeds

1 tbsp (14 ml) freshly squeezed lemon juice

⅓ C (33 g) all-purpose flour

½ C (95 g) granulated sugar

CRUMBLE TOPPING

2 C (198 g) all-purpose flour

1 tbsp (12 g) brown sugar

1 tbsp (12 g) granulated sugar

¼ tsp salt

6 tbsp (86 g) butter, at room temperature

½ tsp vanilla extract

1 large egg white, beaten, for brushing

Preheat the oven to 325°F (162°C). Grease a 9-inch (23 cm)-diameter pie dish, and grease and flour a large baking sheet.

To prepare the filling: Wash and drain the blueberries and pomegranate seeds.

In a medium-size bowl, stir together the blueberries, pomegranate seeds and lemon juice. In a larger bowl, stir together the flour and granulated sugar. Pour the fruit into the flour mixture and stir to coat the fruit. Transfer to the prepared pie dish.

Bake at 325°F (162°C) for 25 to 30 minutes. Remove from the oven and let cool. Increase the oven temperature to 375°F (190°C).

To prepare the topping: In a large mixing bowl, combine all the topping ingredients, except the butter and vanilla. Using a pastry blender or a fork, cut the butter into the mixture until it resembles coarse bread crumbs. Add the vanilla and stir lightly with a fork to distribute it through the mixture.

To assemble the pie pops: Flour both sides of the two piecrusts, then roll flat with a rolling pin. Using a 3-inch (7.6 cm) round cookie cutter, cut twenty-four rounds from the dough, twelve for the bottom crust and twelve for the top crust.

Lay out the twelve bottom crusts on the prepared baking sheet. Brush each bottom crust with egg white, using a silicone basting brush. Press an 8-inch (20 cm)-long cookie stick firmly on top of the center of each bottom crust.

Dispense a 1 ½-inch (about 4 cm) dollop of blueberry-pomegranate filling in the center of each bottom crust. Place a top crust over each bottom crust and press firmly around the sides only, sealing the filling inside.

Create a cookie stick dowel by cutting a 1-inch (2.5 cm)-long piece off the end of an 8-inch (20 cm)-long cookie stick. Use this dowel to crimp the sealed edges of the pie pop by pressing firmly on each side of the stick first, then move counterclockwise around the edges. This will keep the stick from moving around once the pie pop is baked.

After each pop is sealed and pressed, brush more egg white on each top crust. Finally, sprinkle the top crusts with the crumble mixture.

Bake the sheet on the center rack of the oven for 15 to 18 minutes, until the crust is nice and golden. Then place the individual pops on a cooling rack and let cool for at least 15 minutes before serving.

2

Sweet & Sophisticated Pie Pops

Maybe it's the Southern girl in me, but I'm a sucker for sweet and cream-based pies. These are the ones that truly give cakes a run for their money as the dessert of choice. Although they are predominantly similar in their base, you can get very creative with added ingredients. They are great served warm, at room temperature or even slightly chilled.

Traditionally, you find these pies open-faced (meaning they have no top crust); however, for the sake of the pie pop, you will find all my sweet pies enclosed, with additional toppings as the finishing touch.

These pie pops are easily included at seasonal dinner parties or buffets because their toppings can be so creative. The exceptionally unique recipes range from Mint Fudge (page 88; perfect for spring) to Peppermint Pudding (page 73; a new way to enjoy mint candy). If you are making your way through the cookbook, I promise you'll find yourself coming back to this chapter because each pop is so wonderfully distinctive and charming.

Island Banana

After our family trip to the Hawaiian Islands, I was inspired to bring back a little taste of our vacation in the form of a tropical-flavored pie pop. When I think "tropical," I immediately think of bananas and coconuts. I took the liberty of combining the two flavors in a delicate balance and came up with a delightfully sweet and fun pop that is as tasty as it is pretty.

YIELD: 2 DOZEN PIE POPS

---

1 recipe Homemade Pie Pop Crust (page 13), or 4 unbaked store-bought or homemade 9″ (23 cm)-diameter piecrusts

BANANA CUSTARD FILLING

4 large egg yolks (see note)

1 (14 oz [426 ml]) can sweetened condensed milk

1 tsp vanilla extract

2 very ripe bananas

1 large egg white, beaten, for brushing

Sweetened shredded coconut, for garnish

Preheat the oven to 375°F (190°C). Grease and flour a large baking sheet.

To prepare the filling: In a medium-size bowl, beat the egg yolks until frothy. Add condensed milk and vanilla, stirring until well blended.

Blend the bananas to a puree in a food processor. Mix the bananas into the egg mixture and stir well. Pour the banana mixture into a 9-inch (23 cm)-diameter pie dish and bake for 15 to 20 minutes, until a slight crust forms on top. Remove from the oven and let cool to room temperature before using. Keep the oven temperature at 375°F (190°C).

To assemble the pie pops: Flour both sides of the two piecrusts, then roll flat with a rolling pin. Using a 3-inch (7.6 cm) round cookie cutter, cut twenty-four rounds from the dough, twelve for the bottom crust and twelve for the top crust.

Lay out the twelve bottom crusts on the prepared baking sheet. Brush each bottom crust with egg white, using a silicone basting brush. Press an 8-inch (20 cm)-long cookie stick firmly on top of the center of each bottom crust.

Dispense a 1 ½-inch (about 4 cm) dollop of banana filling in the center of each bottom crust. Place a top crust over each bottom crust and press firmly around the sides only, sealing the filling inside.

Create a cookie stick dowel by cutting a 1-inch (2.5 cm)-long piece off the end of an 8-inch (20 cm)-long cookie stick. Use this dowel to crimp the sealed edges of the pie pop by pressing firmly on each side of the stick first, then move counterclockwise around the edges. This will keep the stick from moving around once the pie pop is baked.

(continued)

After each pop is sealed and pressed, brush more egg white on each top crust and, while wet, sprinkle with the coconut.

Bake the sheet on the center rack of the oven for 15 to 18 minutes, until the crust is nice and golden. Then place the individual pops on a cooling rack. Let cool for at least 15 minutes before serving.

Note: You can save the egg whites for brushing pie pops, so don't toss them out!

Raspberry Whip

There is something so light and refreshing about raspberries. They are not overly sweet, so they are easy to pair with richer flavors and often grace the tops of even the most decadent desserts. However, I figured they were due their own pie pop based around their wonderfully fresh aura. This raspberry custard–based pie pop is elegant in taste and finish, and quickly became my go-to favorite to bake when I needed something a little surprising.

YIELD: 2 DOZEN PIE POPS

---

1 recipe Homemade Pie Pop Crust (page 13), or 4 unbaked store-bought or homemade 9″ (23 cm)-diameter piecrusts

RASPBERRY FILLING
2 large eggs
1 ⅓ C (160 g) sour cream
1 tsp vanilla extract
1 C (191 g) granulated sugar
Pinch of salt
⅓ C (33 g) all-purpose flour
4 C (151 g) raspberries

VANILLA GLAZE
1 tsp butter
1 ½ C (195 g) confectioners' sugar
2 tbsp (29 ml) milk or water
¼ tsp vanilla extract

1 large egg white, beaten, for brushing

Preheat the oven to 400°F (204°C). Grease and flour a large baking sheet.

To prepare the filling: In a large bowl, beat the eggs until light and lemon colored. Whisk in the sour cream and vanilla.

In a separate bowl, mix the granulated sugar, salt and flour together; stir into the egg mixture. Gently fold in the raspberries. Pour into a 9-inch (23 cm)-diameter pie dish and bake for 30 to 35 minutes. Remove from the oven and let cool to room temperature. Lower the oven temperature to 375°F (190°C).

To prepare the glaze: Melt the butter, then add all the other ingredients. Stir until creamy. If the glaze is too runny, add more sugar; if it is too thick, add more water ½ tsp at a time.

To assemble the pie pops: Flour both sides of the two piecrusts, then roll flat with a rolling pin. Using a 3-inch (7.6 cm) round cookie cutter, cut twenty-four rounds from the dough, twelve for the bottom crust and twelve for the top crust.

Lay out the twelve bottom crusts on the prepared baking sheet. Brush each bottom crust with egg white, using a silicone basting brush. Press an 8-inch (20 cm)-long cookie stick firmly on top of the center of each bottom crust.

Dispense a 1 ½-inch (about 4 cm) dollop of raspberry filling in the center of each bottom crust. Place a top crust over each bottom crust and press firmly around the sides only, sealing the filling inside.

(continued)

Create a cookie stick dowel by cutting a 1-inch (2.5 cm)-long piece off the end of an 8-inch (20 cm)-long cookie stick. Use this dowel to crimp the sealed edges of the pie pop by pressing firmly on each side of the stick first, then move counterclockwise around the edges. This will keep the stick from moving around once the pie pop is baked.

After each pop is sealed and pressed, brush more egg white on each top crust.

Bake the sheet on the center rack of the oven for 15 to 18 minutes, until the crust is nice and golden. Then place the individual pops on a cooling rack. While they are still warm, drizzle with the glaze in a crisscross motion. Allow to dry completely before handling and let cool for at least 15 minutes before serving.

Pink Lemon Meringue

Fresh pink lemon juice and Meyer lemon zest are what make this pie pop really, well . . . pop! If you can't find pink lemons or if they aren't in season, you can always use a touch of red food dye mixed into the lemon juice to make a pink color, if you wish. It's a great little twist on the standard variety lemon meringue pie. Of course, the meringue is not completely rational in pie pop form, but the fun star shape and confectioners' sugar make for a wonderfully delicate finish, just as you find in a typical meringue. I think you'll come to favor this version!

YIELD: 2 DOZEN PIE POPS

1 recipe Homemade Pie Pop Crust (page 13), or 4 unbaked store-bought or homemade 9″ (23 cm)-diameter piecrusts

LEMON FILLING

1 ½ C (287 g) granulated sugar

3 tbsp (18 g) all-purpose flour

¼ C + 1 tbsp (46 g) cornstarch

¼ tsp salt

2 ¼ C (532 ml) milk

Juice of 3 pink lemons

Zest of 3 Meyer lemons

3 tbsp (43 g) butter

6 large egg yolks (see note)

1 large egg white, beaten, for brushing

Confectioners' sugar, for dusting

To prepare the filling: In a medium-size saucepan, combine the granulated sugar, flour, cornstarch and salt. Stir in the milk, lemon juice and lemon zest and cook over medium-high heat, stirring frequently, until the mixture comes to a boil. Stir in the butter.

Beat the egg yolks in a large bowl. Gradually whisk ½ cup (188 ml) of the hot lemon mixture into the beaten eggs. Whisk the egg mixture back into the sugar mixture in the saucepan and lower the heat to medium-low. Cook, stirring constantly, for 10 to 15 minutes, until thickened.

Remove from the heat and allow to cool to room temperature. Refrigerate the mixture for at least 4 hours, until firm.

Preheat the oven to 375°F (190°C). Grease and flour a large baking sheet.

To assemble the pie pops: Flour both sides of the two piecrusts, then roll flat with a rolling pin. Using a 3 to 4-inch (7.5 to 10 cm) star-shaped cookie cutter, cut twenty-four stars from the dough, twelve for the bottom crust and twelve for the top crust.

Lay out the twelve bottom crusts on the prepared baking sheet. Brush each bottom crust with egg white, using a silicone basting brush. Press an 8-inch (20 cm)-long cookie stick firmly on top of the center of each bottom crust.

Dispense a 1 ½-inch (about 4 cm) dollop of lemon filling in the center of each bottom crust. Place a top crust over each bottom crust and press firmly around the sides only, sealing the filling inside.

(continued)

Create a cookie stick dowel by cutting a 1-inch (2.5 cm)-long piece off the end of an 8-inch (20 cm)-long cookie stick. Use this dowel to crimp the sealed edges of the pie pop by pressing firmly on each side of the stick first, then move counterclockwise around the edges. This will keep the stick from moving around once the pie pop is baked.

After each pop is sealed and pressed, brush more egg white on each top crust.

Bake the sheet on the center rack of the oven for 15 to 18 minutes, until the crust is nice and golden. Then place the individual pops on a cooling rack. Sift confectioners' sugar on top of each crust. Let cool for at least 15 minutes before serving.

Note: You can save the egg whites for brushing pie pops, so don't toss them out!

Pumpkin Cheesecake

While classic pumpkin pie is definitely a favorite holiday treat for most, Pumpkin Cheesecake pie pops are quickly taking over! There's something about the creaminess of the pumpkin with the subtle sourness of the cream cheese that really takes these pops to a whole new level. A little pumpkin goes a long way, so have these perfectly-portioned pie pops featured at your next holiday gathering. Their size and mobility definitely make them the perfect dessert-on-the-go for your guests during the hustle and bustle.

YIELD: 2 DOZEN PIE POPS

---

1 recipe Homemade Pie Pop Crust (page 13), or 4 unbaked store-bought or homemade 9" (23 cm)-diameter piecrusts

PUMPKIN CHEESECAKE FILLING
16 oz (453 g) cream cheese, softened
½ C (90 g) canned pure pumpkin puree
½ C (96 g) granulated sugar
½ tsp vanilla extract
½ tsp ground cinnamon
⅛ tsp ground nutmeg
Pinch of ground cloves
2 large eggs

1 large egg white, beaten, for brushing
1 (6 oz [170 g]) bag sliced almonds, for garnish
Coarse sugar, for garnish

Preheat the oven to 350°F (176°C).

To prepare the filling: Combine the cream cheese, pumpkin, granulated sugar, vanilla and spices; mix with an electric mixer on medium speed until well blended. Add the eggs and mix until blended. Pour into a 9-inch (23 cm)-diameter pie dish and bake at 350°F (176°C) for 35 to 45 minutes, or until set.

Remove from the oven and let cool to room temperature, then refrigerate for at least 3 hours (or overnight). Preheat the oven to 375°F (190°C). Grease and flour a large baking sheet.

To assemble the pie pops: Flour both sides of the two piecrusts, then roll flat with a rolling pin. Using a 3-inch (7.6 cm) round cookie cutter, cut twenty-four rounds from the dough, twelve for the bottom crust and twelve for the top crust.

Lay out the twelve bottom crusts on the prepared baking sheet. Brush each bottom crust with egg white, using a silicone basting brush. Press an 8-inch (20 cm)-long cookie stick firmly on top of the center of each bottom crust.

Dispense a 1 ½-inch (about 4 cm) dollop of pumpkin cheesecake pie filling in the center of each bottom crust. Place a top crust over each bottom crust and press firmly around the sides only, sealing the filling inside.

(continued)

Create a cookie stick dowel by cutting a 1-inch (2.5 cm)-long piece off the end of an 8-inch (20 cm)-long cookie stick. Use this dowel to crimp the sealed edges of the pie pop by pressing firmly on each side of the stick first, then move counterclockwise around the edges. This will keep the stick from moving around once the pie pop is baked.

After each pop is sealed and pressed, brush more egg white on each top crust. While the crusts are still wet, gently press five sliced almonds in starlike pattern on each top crust. Finally, sprinkle the top crusts with coarse sugar.

Bake the sheet on the center rack of the oven for 15 to 18 minutes, until the crust is nice and golden. Then place the individual pops on a cooling rack. Let cool for at least 15 minutes before serving.

Key West Lime

You don't have to go to Florida for the perfect Key lime pie and you don't need to prepare an entire pie to enjoy Key lime! These tasty little pops boast all that tangy lime filling of their larger counterpart, and I've kept this recipe simple so you can whip these up fast! I've had even the toughest-to-please customers tell me that this remains their all-time favorite pie pop because they stay so moist and sweet, even days after baking.

YIELD: 2 DOZEN PIE POPS

1 recipe Homemade Pie Pop Crust (page 13), or 4 unbaked store-bought or homemade 9″ (23 cm)-diameter piecrusts

KEY LIME FILLING

4 large egg yolks (see note)

1 (14 oz [426 ml]) can sweetened condensed milk

Zest from 5 Key limes (the darker green, the better)

1 drop green food dye (optional)

½ C (118 ml) freshly squeezed Key lime juice (15 to 20 Key limes)

VANILLA GLAZE

1 tsp butter

1 ½ C (195 g) confectioners' sugar

2 tbsp (29 ml) milk or water

¼ tsp vanilla extract

1 large egg white, beaten, for brushing

Preheat the oven to 375°F (190°C). Grease and flour a large baking sheet.

To prepare the filling: Beat the egg yolks in a medium-size mixing bowl for about 2 minutes. Add the sweetened condensed milk and stir in the grated lime zest. In a separate small bowl, add the green food dye, if using, to the lime juice and blend until dissolved. Add the juice to the egg mixture and mix thoroughly.

Pour into a 9-inch (23 cm)-diameter pie dish and bake for 20 minutes, until set. Let cool to room temperature. Keep the oven temperature at 375°F (190°C).

To prepare the glaze: Melt the butter, then add all the other ingredients. Stir until creamy. If the glaze is too runny, add more sugar; if it is too thick, add more water ½ tsp at a time.

To assemble the pie pops: Flour both sides of the two piecrusts, then roll flat with a rolling pin. Using a 3-inch (7.6 cm) round cookie cutter, cut twenty-four rounds from the dough, twelve for the bottom crust and twelve for the top crust.

Lay out the twelve bottom crusts on the prepared baking sheet. Brush each bottom crust with egg white, using a silicone basting brush. Press an 8-inch (20 cm)-long cookie stick firmly on top of the center of each bottom crust.

Dispense a 1 ½-inch (about 4 cm) dollop of Key lime filling in the center of each bottom crust. Place a top crust over each bottom crust and press firmly around the sides only, sealing the filling inside.

If you can't find Key limes, you can use ¼ cup (60 ml) of Persian lime juice plus ¼ cup (60 ml) of freshly squeezed lemon juice.

(continued)

Create a cookie stick dowel by cutting a 1-inch (2.5 cm)-long piece off the end of an 8-inch (20 cm)-long cookie stick. Use this dowel to crimp the sealed edges of the pie pop by pressing firmly on each side of the stick first, then move counterclockwise around the edges. This will keep the stick from moving around once the pie pop is baked.

After each pop is sealed and pressed, brush more egg white on each top crust.

Bake the sheet on the center rack of the oven for 15 to 18 minutes, until the crust is nice and golden. Then place the individual pops on a cooling rack. While they are still warm, brush the glaze over the top of each crust. Allow to dry completely before handling and let cool for at least 15 minutes before serving.

Note: You can save the egg whites for brushing pie pops, so don't toss them out!

Mississippi Mud

This is my own version of the classic Mississippi Mud. Because I consider myself a Southern girl, I'm allowed to bend the rules on this one. This Southern dandy pop requires a bit of patience and maybe a little practice, but it's definitely worth it. The trick is layering (just as with the original pie). We are not going to add the whipped topping layer, as these pops are baked and not chilled, but with the dark chocolate glaze and coconut-pecan topping, you'll hardly miss it.

YIELD: 2 DOZEN PIE POPS

1 recipe Homemade Pie Pop Crust (page 13), or 4 unbaked store-bought or homemade 9″ (23 cm)-diameter piecrusts

"MUD" FILLING

½ C (114 g) butter, melted

½ C (49 g) all-purpose flour

1 C (120 g) finely chopped pecans

4 oz (113 g) cream cheese, softened

½ C (65 g) confectioners' sugar

1 tsp vanilla extract

8 oz (226 g) semisweet chocolate chips

DARK CHOCOLATE GLAZE

1 tsp butter

1 ½ C (195 g) confectioners' sugar

2 tbsp (29 ml) milk or water

2 tbsp (28 g) unsweetened cocoa powder

¼ tsp vanilla extract

1 large egg white, beaten, for brushing

½ C (38 g) sweetened shredded coconut, for garnish

½ C (60 g) finely chopped pecans, for garnish

Preheat the oven to 375°F (190°C). Grease and flour a large baking sheet.

To prepare the filling: In a small bowl, combine the melted butter with the flour and mix well, then add the pecans. Stir until the pecans are coated with the flour mixture.

In another bowl, mix together the cream cheese, confectioners' sugar and vanilla; beat with an electric mixture, at medium speed, until well blended.

Using a double boiler, melt the chocolate chips over medium heat. Once the chocolate is smooth, add the pecan mixture, stir, then remove from the heat.

To prepare the glaze: Melt the butter, then add all the other ingredients. Stir until creamy. If the glaze is too runny, add more sugar; if it is too thick, add more water ½ tsp at a time.

To assemble the pie pops: Flour both sides of the two piecrusts, then roll flat with a rolling pin. Using a 3-inch (7.6 cm) round cookie cutter, cut twenty-four rounds from the dough, twelve for the bottom crust and twelve for the top crust.

Lay out the bottom crusts on the prepared baking sheet. Brush each bottom crust with egg white, using a silicone basting brush. Press an 8-inch (20 cm)-long cookie stick firmly on top of the center of each bottom crust. Layer both mixtures, starting with about 1 teaspoon of the chocolate mixture on the bottom and then 1 teaspoon of the cream cheese mixture on top, centered on each bottom crust, being careful not to overfill each pop. Place a top crust over each bottom crust and press firmly around the sides only, sealing the filling inside.

(continued)

Create a cookie stick dowel by cutting a 1-inch (2.5 cm)-long piece off the end of an 8-inch (20 cm)-long cookie stick. Use this dowel to crimp the sealed edges of the pie pop by pressing firmly on each side of the stick first, then move counterclockwise around the edges. This will keep the stick from moving around once the pie pop is baked.

After each pop is sealed and pressed, brush more egg white on each top crust.

Bake the sheet on the center rack of the oven for 15 to 18 minutes, until the crust is nice and golden. Then place the individual pops on a cooling rack. While they are still warm, brush the glaze over the top of each crust; then, while the glaze is still wet, sprinkle with the coconut and pecans. Allow to dry completely before handling.

Crème Brûlée

While this version of a favorite French dessert forgoes the ramekins and torches, it doesn't opt out on presentation. The key to success for this little pop lies with the touch of Amaretto and the sparkle of the caramelized sugar topping. You can also use brown sugar as a substitute if you have a hard time finding the sugar crystals. Now, you can enjoy crème brûlée on the go!

YIELD: 2 DOZEN PIE POPS

---

1 recipe Homemade Pie Pop Crust (page 13), or 4 unbaked store-bought or homemade 9" (23 cm)-diameter piecrusts

VANILLA CRÈME FILLING

½ C (95 g) granulated sugar

¼ C (24 g) all-purpose flour

½ tsp salt

2 C (473 ml) milk

2 large egg yolks, lightly beaten (see note)

1 tbsp (14 ml) Amaretto

2 tsp vanilla extract

CARAMEL GLAZE

4 tbsp (57 g) butter, cut up

½ C (110 g) light brown sugar, packed

⅓ C (78 ml) whipping cream

¼ tsp salt

1 C (130 g) confectioners' sugar, or as needed

1 large egg white, beaten, for brushing

Coarse sugar crystals or gold cupcake sprinkles

Preheat the oven to 375°F (190°C). Grease and flour a large baking sheet.

To prepare the filling: In a small saucepan, combine the granulated sugar, flour and salt. Stir in the milk until smooth. Cook and stir over medium-high heat until thickened and bubbly, then lower the heat and cook, stirring, for 2 more minutes.

Remove from the heat and stir ¼ cup (59 ml) of the hot filling into a medium-sized bowl. Add the beaten egg yolks. Return the mixture to the saucepan. Bring back to a gentle boil, stir in the Amaretto, and stirring constantly, cook for 2 more minutes. Remove from the heat and gently stir in the vanilla. Let cool to room temperature.

To prepare the glaze: Place the butter into a medium-size saucepan with the brown sugar, cream and salt and cook over medium heat until bubbly, stirring constantly.

Bring to a full boil; cook, stirring, for 1 minute; then remove from the heat. Once cooled slightly, add enough confectioners' sugar to achieve a thick but pourable consistency.

To assemble the pie pops: Flour both sides of the two piecrusts, then roll flat with a rolling pin. Using a 3-inch (7.6 cm) round cookie cutter, cut twenty-four rounds from the dough, twelve for the bottom crust and v for the top crust.

Lay out the twelve bottom crusts on the prepared baking sheet. Brush each bottom crust with egg white, using a silicone basting brush. Press an 8-inch (20 cm)-long cookie stick firmly on top of the center of each bottom crust.

(continued)

Dispense a 1 ½-inch (about 4 cm) dollop of vanilla crème filling in the center of each bottom crust. Place a top crust over each bottom crust and press firmly around the sides only, sealing the filling inside.

Create a cookie stick dowel by cutting a 1-inch (2.5 cm)-long piece off the end of an 8-inch (20 cm)-long cookie stick. Use this dowel to crimp the sealed edges of the pie pop by pressing firmly on each side of the stick first, then move counterclockwise around the edges. This will keep the stick from moving around once the pie pop is baked.

After each pop is sealed and pressed, brush more egg white on each top crust.

Bake the sheet on the center rack of the oven for 15 to 18 minutes, until the crust is nice and golden. Then place the individual pops on a cooling rack. While they are still warm, brush each pop with the glaze and sprinkle with coarse sugar or gold sprinkles; let the glaze set before moving. Allow to dry completely before handling.

Note: You can save the egg whites for brushing pie pops, so don't toss them out!

Chocolate Cream

Sometimes you just want chocolate and nothing satisfies your craving like chocolate cream pie. One of the best things about making this rich dessert in the form of a pie pop is that you can have just a little to satisfy your sweet tooth, or three or four. It's really up to you whether you want to share or not! I make my chocolate cream with a touch of cinnamon and salt to really liven up that chocolate flavor and make it unforgettable!

YIELD: 2 DOZEN PIE POPS

---

1 recipe Homemade Pie Pop Crust (page 13), or 4 unbaked store-bought or homemade 9″ (23 cm)-diameter piecrusts

CHOCOLATE CREAM FILLING

1 ⅔ C (394 ml) water

3 tbsp (28 g) cornstarch

5 tbsp (34 g) unsweetened cocoa powder

3 large egg yolks, beaten (see note)

1 (14 oz [385 ml]) can sweetened condensed milk

2 tbsp (28 g) butter

1 tsp vanilla extract

½ tsp ground cinnamon

1 tsp coarse salt

1 large egg white, beaten, for brushing

Confectioners' sugar, for dusting

Preheat the oven to 375°F (190°C). Grease and flour a large baking sheet.

To prepare the filling: In a large saucepan, whisk together the water, cornstarch and cocoa powder until smooth. Place over medium heat. Immediately stir in the egg yolks and condensed milk and cook until thickened, stirring constantly.

Lower the heat to low and stir in the butter until completely combined. Remove from the heat and add the vanilla, cinnamon and salt; mix well. Let cool slightly before using.

To assemble the pie pops: Flour both sides of the two piecrusts, then roll flat with a rolling pin. Using a 3-inch (7.6 cm) round cookie cutter, cut twenty-four rounds from the dough, twelve for the bottom crust and twelve for the top crust.

Lay out the twelve bottom crusts on a large, greased and floured baking sheet. Brush each bottom crust with egg white, using a silicone basting brush. Press an 8-inch (20 cm)-long cookie stick firmly on top of the center of each bottom crust.

Dispense a 1 ½-inch (about 4 cm) dollop of chocolate pie filling in the center of each bottom crust. Place a top crust over each bottom crust and press firmly around the sides only, sealing the filling inside.

Create a cookie stick dowel by cutting a 1-inch (2.5 cm) piece of the end of an 8-inch (20 cm)-long cookie stick. Use this dowel to crimp the sealed edges of the pie pop by pressing firmly on each side of the stick first, then move counterclockwise around the edges. This will keep the stick from moving around once the pie pop is baked.

(continued)

After each pop is sealed and pressed, brush more egg white on each top crust.

Bake the sheet on the center rack of the oven for 15 to 18 minutes, until the crust is nice and golden. Then place the individual pops on a cooling rack. Sift confectioners' sugar on top of each crust. Let cool for at least 15 minutes before serving.

Note: You can save the egg whites for brushing pie pops, so don't toss them out!

Orange Flan

While it is a sidestep from traditional flan, this orange-infused custard makes for a lighter dessert, refreshes the palate and satisfies even the most avid sweet tooth. Be open to enjoy this variation of the Spanish treat and you'll find even your favorites can be enjoyed in the form of a pie pop!

YIELD: 2 DOZEN PIE POPS

1 recipe Homemade Pie Pop Crust (page 13), or 4 unbaked store-bought or homemade 9" (23 cm)-diameter piecrusts

ORANGE FLAN FILLING

3 large egg yolks (see note)

1 (14 oz [385 ml]) can sweetened condensed milk

¼ tsp salt

½ C (118 ml) freshly squeezed orange juice

Zest from 1 orange

1 tsp freshly squeezed lemon juice

CARAMEL-ORANGE GLAZE

4 tbsp (57 g) butter, cut up

½ C (100 g) light brown sugar, packed

⅓ C (78 ml) whipping cream

¼ tsp salt

Zest from 1 medium-size orange

1 C (191 g) confectioners' sugar, or as needed

1 large egg white, beaten, for brushing

Preheat the oven to 375°F (190°C). Grease and flour a large baking sheet.

To prepare the filling: In a small bowl, beat the egg yolks for 1 to 2 minutes. In a large bowl, combine the egg yolks with all the other ingredients by hand until well mixed.

Pour into a 9-inch (23 cm)-diameter pie dish and bake for 20 to 25 minutes, until a thin crust forms on the top. Remove from the oven and let cool to room temperature; use right away. Leave the oven temperature at 375°F (190°C).

To prepare the glaze: Put the butter into a medium-size saucepan with the brown sugar, cream, salt and orange zest and cook over medium heat until bubbly, stirring constantly.

Bring to a full boil; cook, stirring, for 1 minute; then remove from the heat. Once cooled slightly, add enough confectioners' sugar to achieve a thick but pourable consistency.

To assemble the pie pops: Flour both sides of the two piecrusts, then roll flat with a rolling pin. Using a 3-inch (7.6 cm) round cookie cutter, cut twenty-four rounds from the dough, twelve for the bottom crust and twelve for the top crust.

Lay out the twelve bottom crusts on the prepared baking sheet. Brush each bottom crust with egg white, using a silicone basting brush. Press an 8-inch (20 cm)-long cookie stick firmly on top of the center of each bottom crust.

Dispense a 1 ½-inch (about 4 cm) dollop of orange flan filling in the center of each bottom crust. Place a top crust over each bottom crust and press firmly around the sides only, sealing the filling inside.

Create a cookie stick dowel by cutting a 1-inch (2.5 cm)-long piece off the end of an 8-inch (20 cm)-long cookie stick. Use this dowel to crimp the sealed edges of the pie pop by pressing firmly on each side of the stick first, then move counterclockwise around the edges. This will keep the stick from moving around once the pie pop is baked.

After each pop is sealed and pressed, brush more egg white on each top crust.

Bake the sheet on the center rack of the oven for 15 to 18 minutes, until the crust is nice and golden. Then place the individual pops on a cooling rack. While they are still warm, brush each pop with the glaze; let the glaze set before moving. Allow to dry completely before handling.

Note: You can save the egg whites for brushing pie pops, so don't toss them out!

Boston Cream

Boston cream pies are typically more of a cake than a traditional pie; however, I wanted to capture in one of my mini pies that rich decadence that makes this treat so special. The custard is what really brings this dessert to life and the chocolate is definitely the icing on the cake (so to speak). I wanted a bold vanilla flavor, so I use Danncy Mexican Vanilla, but any pure vanilla extract will do the trick. As for the chocolate, you want to get that evenly-thickened glaze that will temper nicely once dried, so the ratio of sugar to chocolate is the key. Even though it's a mini pie, this dessert will surely feel like a full serving!

YIELD: 2 DOZEN PIE POPS

---

1 recipe Homemade Pie Pop Crust (page 13), or 4 unbaked store-bought or homemade 9" (23 cm)-diameter piecrusts

CREAM FILLING
⅓ C (63 g) granulated sugar

2 tbsp (18 g) cornstarch

⅛ tsp salt

1 ½ C (355 ml) whipping cream

2 egg yolks, lightly beaten (see note)

2 tsp (10 ml) vanilla extract

DARK CHOCOLATE GLAZE
1 tsp butter

1 ½ C (195 g) confectioners' sugar

2 tbsp (29 ml) milk or water

2 tbsp (28 g) unsweetened cocoa powder

¼ tsp vanilla extract

1 large egg white, beaten, for brushing

Preheat the oven to 375°F (190°C). Grease and flour a large baking sheet.

To prepare the filling: Mix the granulated sugar, cornstarch and salt in a 2-quart (1.9 L) saucepan. Whisk in the cream gradually (½ cup [118 ml] at a time), cooking over medium heat and stirring constantly, until the mixture thickens and boils. Boil, stirring, for 1 minute.

Add the egg yolks to the hot mixture, bring back to a boil, then boil, stirring, for 1 minute. Remove from the heat and stir in the vanilla. Let cool to room temperature.

To prepare the glaze: Melt the butter, and then add all the other ingredients. Stir until creamy. If the glaze is too runny, add more sugar; if it is too thick, add more water ½ tsp at a time.

To assemble the pie pops: Flour both sides of the two piecrusts, then roll flat with a rolling pin. Using a 3-inch (7.6 cm) round cookie cutter, cut twenty-four rounds from the dough, twelve for the bottom crust and twelve for the top crust.

Lay out the twelve bottom crusts on the prepared baking sheet. Brush each bottom crust with egg white, using a silicone basting brush. Press an 8-inch (20 cm)-long cookie stick firmly on top of the center of each bottom crust.

Dispense a 1 ½-inch (about 4 cm) dollop of cream filling in the center of each bottom crust. Place a top crust over each bottom crust and press firmly around the sides only, sealing the filling inside.

(continued)

Create a cookie stick dowel by cutting a 1-inch (2.5 cm)-long piece off the end of an 8-inch (20 cm)-long cookie stick. Use this dowel to crimp the sealed edges of the pie pop by pressing firmly on each side of the stick first, then move counterclockwise around the edges. This will keep the stick from moving around once the pie pop is baked.

After each pop is sealed and pressed, brush more egg white on each top crust.

Bake the sheet on the center rack of the oven for 15 to 18 minutes, until the crust is nice and golden. Then place the individual pops on a cooling rack. While they are still warm, brush each pop with the glaze; let the glaze set before moving. Allow to dry completely before handling.

Note: You can save the egg whites for brushing pie pops, so don't toss them out!

Peppermint Pudding

Peppermint candies are universally loved and easy to find year-round, but the fresh minty taste definitely inspires a holiday treat. Soft peppermints, such as Bob's Sweet Stripe Mint Candy, work best for melting, but if you can't find the soft ones, hard peppermints can be substituted; you'll just have to crush them up beforehand. Either way, this pie is easy, cost effective and festive for that special time of year.

YIELD: 2 DOZEN PIE POPS

---

1 recipe Homemade Pie Pop Crust (page 13), or 4 unbaked store-bought or homemade 9" (23 cm)-diameter piecrusts

PIE FILLING

1 (0.25 oz [7.2 g]) envelope unflavored gelatin

¼ C (59 ml) cold water

2 C (241 g) whipping cream

8 oz (226 g) soft peppermint candy (e.g., Bob's Sweet Stripe Mint Candy)

VANILLA GLAZE

1 tsp butter

1 ½ C (195 g) confectioners' sugar

2 tbsp (29 ml) milk or water

¼ tsp vanilla extract

1 large egg white, beaten, for brushing

Crushed peppermint hard candy, for garnish

To prepare the filling: In a small bowl, add the gelatin to the cold water to soften; set aside. Put ½ cup (60 g) of the cream in a small saucepan with the soft peppermint candy and cook over low heat until the candy melts. Add the gelatin mixture, mix well, then remove from the heat and allow to cool.

In a separate bowl, whip the remaining 1 ½ cups (181 g) of cream. Once the candy mixture is cool, fold the whipped cream into the candy mixture. Chill for 1 hour or until firm. Preheat the oven to 375°F (190°C). Grease and flour a large baking sheet.

To prepare the glaze: Melt the butter, then add all the other ingredients. Stir until creamy. If the glaze is too runny, add more sugar; if it is too thick add more water ½ tsp at a time.

To assemble the pie pops: Flour both sides of the two piecrusts, then roll flat with a rolling pin. Using a 3-inch (7.6 cm) round cookie cutter, cut twenty-four rounds from the dough, twelve for the bottom crust and twelve for the top crust.

Lay out the twelve bottom crusts on the prepared baking sheet. Brush each bottom crust with egg white, using a silicone basting brush. Press an 8-inch (20 cm)-long cookie stick firmly on top of the center of each bottom crust.

Dispense a 1 ½-inch (about 4 cm) dollop of peppermint filling in the center of each bottom crust. Place a top crust over each bottom crust and press firmly around the sides only, sealing the filling inside.

(continued)

Create a cookie stick dowel by cutting a 1-inch (2.5 cm)-long piece off the end of an 8-inch (20 cm)-long cookie stick. Use this dowel to crimp the sealed edges of the pie pop by pressing firmly on each side of the stick first, then move counterclockwise around the edges. This will keep the stick from moving around once the pie pop is baked.

After each pop is sealed and pressed, brush more egg white on each top crust.

Bake the sheet on the center rack of the oven for 15 to 18 minutes, until the crust is nice and golden. Then place the individual pops on a cooling rack. While they are still warm, brush each top crust with the glaze and sprinkle with crushed hard peppermint candies; let the glaze set before moving.

English Toffee

Toffee itself is a great indulgence but toffee in a pie is even better, and these pops highlight this buttery candy inside and out. Although a simple toffee pie might be overshadowed by a plethora of other desserts at an event or celebration, these toffee pie pops can be festively wrapped, tied and displayed upright, so they are sure to never be missed or passed up!

YIELD: 2 DOZEN PIE POPS

1 recipe Homemade Pie Pop Crust (page 13), or 4 unbaked store-bought or homemade 9" (23 cm)-diameter piecrusts

TOFFEE PIE FILLING

1 tbsp (13 g) unflavored gelatin

¼ C (59 ml) cold water

1 C (236 ml) milk

3 large egg yolks (reserve the last white for brushing the pops)

½ C (100 g) light brown sugar

2 tbsp (28 g) butter

1 tsp vanilla extract

2 large egg whites

½ C (118 ml) whipping cream

VANILLA GLAZE

1 tsp butter

1 ½ C (195 g) confectioners' sugar

2 tbsp (29 ml) milk or water

¼ tsp vanilla extract

TOFFEE CANDY TOPPING

½ C (114 g) salted butter

1 C (191 g) granulated sugar

½ tsp vanilla

¼ tsp salt

¼ C (21 g) sliced almonds

1 large egg white, beaten, for brushing

To prepare the filling: In a small bowl, add the gelatin to the cold water to soften for 5 minutes. Using a double boiler, scald the milk in the top pan over boiling water.

In a large bowl, beat the egg yolks well. Add to the milk, along with the brown sugar. Cook until thickened, stirring constantly. Remove from the heat. Add the gelatin, butter and vanilla, mixing well, then set aside to cool.

In another mixing bowl, beat the two egg whites until stiff peaks form. When the milk mixture has cooled, fold in the egg whites.

Beat the cream until stiff and fold into the toffee mixture. Pour into a 9-inch (23 cm)-diameter pie dish and chill for 1 hour, or until firm.

Preheat the oven to 375°F (190°C). Grease and flour a large baking sheet.

(continued)

To prepare the glaze: Melt the butter, then add all the other ingredients. Stir until creamy. If the glaze is too runny, add more sugar; if it is too thick add more water ½ tsp at a time.

To prepare the topping: Grease an 8-inch (20 cm) square pan.

In a nonstick skillet, melt the butter over medium heat. Once the butter is melted, add the granulated sugar and stir continually with a wooden spoon until the mixture bubbles and gradually turns golden brown (5 to 6 minutes).

Remove from the heat and immediately stir in the vanilla and salt. Quickly transfer to the greased pan and even out with a spoon. Before the toffee sets, sprinkle the sliced almonds on top and gently press into the toffee with your hand (you may want to cover your hand with a plastic bag), but be careful—the toffee is hot! Allow to cool. Once completely cooled, break into very small pieces to use for the pie pop topping.

To assemble the pie pops: Flour both sides of the two piecrusts, then roll flat with a rolling pin. Using a 3-inch (7.6 cm) round cookie cutter, cut twenty-four rounds from the dough, twelve for the bottom crust and twelve for the top crust.

Lay out the twelve bottom crusts on the prepared baking sheet. Brush each bottom crust with egg white, using a silicone basting brush. Press an 8-inch (20 cm)-long cookie stick firmly on top of the center of each bottom crust.

Dispense a 1-½ inch (about 4 cm) dollop of toffee filling in the center of each bottom crust. Place a top crust over each bottom crust and press firmly around the sides only, sealing the filling inside.

Create a cookie stick dowel by cutting a 1-inch (2.5 cm)-long piece off the end of an 8-inch (20 cm)-long cookie stick. Use this dowel to crimp the sealed edges of the pie pop by pressing firmly on each side of the stick first, then move counterclockwise around the edges. This will keep the stick from moving around once the pie pop is baked.

After each pop is sealed and pressed, brush more egg white on each top crust.

Bake the sheet on the center rack of the oven for 15 to 18 minutes, until the crust is nice and golden. Then place the individual pops on a cooling rack. While they are still warm, brush each pop with the glaze. While the glaze is still wet, sprinkle the toffee topping on the tops of the glazed crusts. Let the glaze set and allow to dry completely before handling.

Note: The Toffee Candy Topping makes ½ pound.

Persimmon Spice

I had never even tasted a persimmon until my husband brought one home from work one day (he works in produce). At first sight, I didn't think much of it at all; it almost resembled an underripe tomato. However, once I bit into it, I felt as if I were eating a piece of Christmas off the tree! It's got a spicy and sweet flavor that I immediately knew I wanted to incorporate into one of my pie pops. The flesh of the fruit bakes beautifully and is so amazing on its own that you won't need much else to make this one of your favorite pies to enjoy at Christmastime or year-round!

YIELD: 2 DOZEN PIE POPS

---

1 recipe Homemade Pie Pop Crust (page 13), or 4 unbaked store-bought or homemade 9″ (23 cm)-diameter piecrusts

PERSIMMON PIE FILLING

2 large eggs

½ tsp ground cinnamon

¼ tsp ground cloves

½ C (95 g) granulated sugar

⅓ tsp salt

2 C (473 ml) whipping cream

1 C (180 g) persimmon pulp (puree)

2 tbsp (28 g) butter, melted

1 tsp freshly squeezed lemon juice

1 tsp vanilla extract

1 large egg white, beaten, for brushing

1:1 mixture of coarse sugar and ground nutmeg, for garnish

Preheat the oven to 450°F (232°C). Grease and flour a large baking sheet.

To prepare the filling: In a large mixing bowl, combine the eggs, cinnamon, cloves, granulated sugar and salt. Stir in the cream, persimmon pulp, melted butter, lemon juice and vanilla.

Pour into a 9-inch (23 cm)-diameter pie dish. Bake for 10 minutes, then lower the oven temperature to 350°F (176°C) and bake for an additional 40 minutes. Allow to cool to room temperature; use right away. Increase the oven temperature to 375°F (190°C).

To assemble the pie pops: Flour both sides of the two piecrusts, then roll flat with a rolling pin. Using a 3-inch (7.6 cm) round cookie cutter, cut twenty-four rounds from the dough, twelve for the bottom crust and twelve for the top crust.

Lay out the twelve bottom crusts on a large, greased and floured baking sheet. Brush each bottom crust with egg white, using a silicone basting brush. Press an 8-inch (20 cm)-long cookie stick firmly on top of the center of each bottom crust.

Dispense a 1 ½-inch (about 4 cm) dollop of persimmon spice filling in the center of each bottom crust. Place a top crust over each bottom crust and press firmly around the sides only, sealing the filling inside.

(continued)

Create a cookie stick dowel by cutting a 1-inch (2.5 cm)-long piece off the end of an 8-inch (20 cm)-long cookie stick. Use this dowel to crimp the sealed edges of the pie pop by pressing firmly on each side of the stick first, then move counterclockwise around the edges. This will keep the stick from moving around once the pie pop is baked.

After each pop is sealed and pressed, brush more egg white on each top crust. Finally, sprinkle the top crusts with the nutmeg sugar.

Bake the sheet on the center rack of the oven for 15 to 18 minutes, until the crust is nice and golden. Then place the individual pops on a cooling rack. Let cool for at least 15 minutes before serving.

Black Forest

Black Forest cake has layers of chocolate cake, whipped cream and cherries. This pie pop features all the flavor of its German ancestor, including the rich chocolate and tart cherries.

YIELD: 2 DOZEN PIE POPS

1 recipe Homemade Pie Pop Crust (page 13), or 4 unbaked store-bought or homemade 9" (23 cm)-diameter piecrusts

BLACK FOREST PIE FILLING

2 tbsp (12 g) all-purpose flour

¾ C (143 g) granulated sugar

½ C (103 g) unsweetened cocoa powder

⅓ C (78 ml) milk

¼ C (57 g) butter, cubed

2 large eggs, lightly beaten

12 oz (340 g) Cherry Tart filling (page 16), or store-bought

1 large egg white, beaten, for brushing

Confectioners' sugar, for brushing

Preheat the oven to 350°F (176°C). Grease and flour a large baking sheet.

To prepare the filling: In a small saucepan, combine the flour, granulated sugar and cocoa; stir in the milk until smooth. Add the butter. Cook, stirring, over medium-high heat until thickened and bubbly.

Lower the heat and cook, stirring, for 2 minutes longer. Remove from the heat; stir a small amount of hot filling into the eggs, then return the mixture to the saucepan, stirring constantly. Fold in the Cherry Tart filling. Pour into a 9-inch (23 cm)-diameter pie dish and bake for 35 to 40 minutes, or until the filling is set. Allow to cool to room temperature; use right away. Increase the oven temperature to 375°F (190°C).

To assemble the pie pops: Flour both sides of the two piecrusts, then roll flat with a rolling pin. Using a 3-inch (7.6 cm) round cookie cutter, cut twenty-four rounds, twelve for the bottom crust and twelve for the top crust.

Lay out the twelve bottom crusts on the prepared baking sheet. Brush each bottom crust with egg white, using a silicone basting brush. Press an 8-inch (20 cm)-long cookie stick firmly on top of the center of each bottom crust.

Dispense a 1 ½-inch (about 4 cm) dollop of Black Forest filling in the center of each bottom crust. Place a top crust over each bottom crust and press firmly around the sides only, sealing the filling inside.

Create a cookie stick dowel by cutting a 1-inch (2.5 cm)-long piece off the end of a cookie stick and use it to crimp the sealed edges of the pie pop by pressing firmly on each side of the stick first, then move counterclockwise around the edges. This will keep the stick from moving around once the pie pop is baked. After each pop is sealed and pressed, brush more egg white on each top crust.

Bake the sheet in the center rack of the oven for 15 to 18 minutes, until the crust is nice and golden. Place the individual pops on a cooling rack, then sift confectioners' sugar on top of each crust. Let cool for at least 15 minutes before serving.

Date Night

I recently fell in love with dates. No, not the dinner-and-a-movie-kind of date, but the chewy, sweet and melt-in-your-mouth, sun-dried palm dates. These date pie pops are a great way to sample these exquisite fruits and are sure to be the talk of the party at any event at which you feature them. Give the exotic a try in your own kitchen.

YIELD: 2 DOZEN PIE POPS

1 recipe Homemade Pie Pop Crust (page 13), or 4 unbaked store-bought or homemade 9" (23 cm)-diameter piecrusts

DATE PIE FILLING

¼ C (57 g) butter, at room temperature

½ C (100 g) light brown sugar, packed

1 large egg

2 tbsp (29 ml) honey

⅛ tsp salt

1 tsp ground cinnamon

½ C (58 g) chopped walnuts

¼ C (37 g) pitted and chopped dried dates

1 large egg white, beaten, for brushing

1:1 mixture of coarse sugar and ground cinnamon, for garnish

Preheat the oven to 375°F (190°C). Grease and flour a large baking sheet.

To prepare the filling: In a mixing bowl, beat the butter with the brown sugar with an electric mixer, at medium speed, until light and fluffy. Beat in the egg, honey, salt and cinnamon. Fold in the walnuts and dates. Use the mixture for the pie pop filling right away.

To assemble the pie pops: Flour both sides of the two piecrusts, then roll flat with a rolling pin. Using a 3-inch (7.6 cm) round cookie cutter, cut twenty-four rounds from the dough, twelve for the bottom crust and twelve for the top crust.

Lay out the twelve bottom crusts on a large, greased and floured baking sheet. Brush each bottom crust with egg white, using a silicone basting brush. Press an 8-inch (20 cm)-long cookie stick firmly on top of the center of each bottom crust.

Dispense a 1 ½-inch (about 4 cm) dollop of date filling in the center of each bottom crust. Place a top crust over each bottom crust and press firmly around the sides only, sealing the filling inside.

Create a cookie stick dowel by cutting a 1-inch (2.5 cm)-long piece off the end of an 8-inch (20 cm)-long cookie stick. Use this dowel to crimp the sealed edges of the pie pop by pressing firmly on each side of the stick first, then move counterclockwise around the edges. This will keep the stick from moving around once the pie pop is baked.

After each pop is sealed and pressed, brush more egg white on each top crust, and sprinkle with cinnamon sugar.

Bake the sheet on the center rack of the oven for 15 to 18 minutes, until the crust is nice and golden. Then place the individual pops on a cooling rack and let cool for at least 15 minutes before serving.

Texas Pecan

There is a saying that everything is bigger is Texas . . . and while this pie pop may not be big in stature, it's definitely made better because of the extra-large, Southern-grown pecans. While I was growing up, my dad's favorite dessert was always pecan pie. In fact, my mom would make an entire pie just for him to enjoy during the holidays. As my parents live on a pecan farm in East Texas, it became my goal as a baker to take my share of the "pecan inheritance" and make one of the best pecan pie recipes I could . . . and I think I've done it! This is also why I use a heart-shaped crust: This pop is so near to my heart. The filling uses absolutely no corn syrup, which allows the robust flavor of the hearty pecans to really stand out. Enjoy, y'all.

YIELD: 2 DOZEN PIE POPS

1 recipe Homemade Pie Pop Crust (page 13), or 4 unbaked store-bought or homemade 9" (23 cm)-diameter piecrusts

PECAN FILLING

2 large eggs

½ C (114 g) butter, melted

1 C (201 g) light brown sugar

¼ C (48 g) granulated sugar

1 tbsp (6 g) all-purpose flour

1 tbsp (14 ml) milk

1 tsp vanilla extract

1 C (120 g) chopped pecans

1 large egg white, beaten, for brushing

1:1 mixture of coarse sugar and ground cinnamon, for garnish

Preheat the oven to 350°F (176°C). Grease and flour a large baking sheet.

To prepare the filling: In a large bowl, beat the eggs until foamy, then stir in the melted butter. Stir in the brown sugar, granulated sugar and flour; mix well. Add the milk, vanilla and pecans; stir well.

Pour directly into a 9-inch(23 cm)-diameter pie dish and bake for 10 minutes, then lower the oven temperature to 300°F (148°C) and bake for 30 minutes until set. Let cool to room temperature before using. Increase oven temperature to 375°F (190°C).

To assemble the pie pops: Flour both sides of the two piecrusts, then roll flat with a rolling pin. Using a 3- to 4–inch (7.5 to 10 cm) heart-shaped cookie cutter, cut twenty-four hearts from the dough, twelve for the bottom crust and twelve for the top crust.

Lay out the twelve bottom crusts on the prepared baking sheet. Brush each bottom crust with egg white, using a silicone basting brush. Press an 8-inch (20 cm)-long cookie stick firmly on top of the center of each bottom crust.

Dispense a 1 ½-inch (about 4 cm) dollop of pecan pie filling in the center of each bottom crust. Place a top crust over each bottom crust and press firmly around the sides the heart only, sealing the filling inside.

(continued)

Create a cookie stick dowel by cutting a 1-inch (2.5 cm)-long piece off the end of an 8-inch (20 cm)-long cookie stick. Use this dowel to crimp the sealed edges of the pie pop by pressing firmly on each side of the stick first, then move counterclockwise around the edges. This will keep the stick from moving around once the pie pop is baked.

After each pop is sealed and pressed, brush more egg whites on each top crust. Finally, sprinkle the top crusts with the cinnamon sugar.

Bake the sheet on the center rack of the oven for 15 to 18 minutes, until the crust is nice and golden. Then place the individual pops on a cooling rack and let cool for at least 15 minutes before serving.

Coconut Cream

Coconut cream pie is a beautiful way to feature this amazing fruit. It looks delicate, tastes tropical and creamy, and is fantastically simple to whip up! I've always been tempted to grate fresh coconut and sweeten it myself, but the commercially-sold shredded variety works well for coconut cream on the go, which is the main theme behind baking pie pops. The ginger is an unexpected touch that really sets the crust apart and adds just the right amount of spice.

YIELD: 2 DOZEN PIE POPS

1 recipe Homemade Pie Pop Crust (page 13), or 4 unbaked store-bought or homemade 9" (23 cm)-diameter piecrusts

COCONUT CREAM FILLING
3 C (709 ml) half-and-half

2 large egg yolks (see note)

½ C (95 g) granulated sugar

⅓ C (50 g) cornstarch

2 tbsp (28 g) butter

1 tsp vanilla extract

1 C (75 g) sweetened shredded coconut

GINGER-COCONUT CRUMBLE
30 gingersnap cookies

¼ C (19 g) sweetened shredded coconut

5 tbsp (71 g) butter, melted

1 large egg white, beaten, for brushing

Preheat the oven to 375°F (190°C). Grease and flour a large baking sheet.

To prepare the filling: In a large saucepan, whisk together (without heating) the half-and-half, egg yolks, granulated sugar and cornstarch until smooth. Place the pan over medium heat and simmer, stirring constantly, until the mixture thickens.

Once thickened, remove from the heat and add the butter, vanilla and shredded coconut. Let cool slightly before using.

To prepare the topping: Pulse the gingersnap cookies in a food processor until they are fine crumbs. Place in a bowl along with the coconut and melted butter; toss to combine. Use for the pie pop topping immediately.

To assemble the pie pops: Flour both sides of the two piecrusts, then roll flat with a rolling pin. Using a 3-inch (7.6 cm) round cookie cutter, cut twenty-four rounds from the dough, twelve for the bottom crust and twelve for the top crust.

Lay out the twelve bottom crusts on the prepared baking sheet. Brush each bottom crust with egg white, using a silicone basting brush. Press an 8-inch (20 cm)-long cookie stick firmly on top of the center of each bottom crust.

Dispense a 1 ½-inch (about 4 cm) dollop of coconut cream filling in the center of each bottom crust. Place a top crust over each bottom crust and press firmly around the sides only, sealing the filling inside.

Create a cookie stick dowel by cutting a 1-inch (2.5 cm)-long piece off the end of an 8-inch (20 cm)-long cookie stick. Use this dowel to crimp the sealed edges of the pie pop by pressing firmly on each side of the stick first, then move counterclockwise around the edges. This will keep the stick from moving around once the pie pop is baked.

After each pop is sealed and pressed, brush more egg white on each top crust. While still wet, sprinkle each top crust with crumbled cookie mixture.

Bake the sheet on the center rack of the oven for 15 to 18 minutes, until the crust is nice and golden. Then place the individual pops on a cooling rack. Let cool for at least 15 minutes before serving.

Note: You can save the egg whites for brushing pie pops, so don't toss them out!

Mint Fudge

Many flavors pair well with chocolate and mint is one of best. The freshness of the mint with the decadence of the dark chocolate fudge . . . yum, that's all there really is to it! I have used fresh mint to make my mint extract before, but for time's sake, my recipe calls for the store-bought variety. It works just as well to include that woodsy, refreshing addition. Being a very visual person, I like to add a drop or two of green food coloring (natural varieties are available) to the glaze as well! This pop makes a perfect treat when you need that bit of color, and would be ideal for spring or St. Paddy's Day!

YIELD: 2 DOZEN PIE POPS

---

1 recipe Homemade Pie Pop Crust (page 13), or 4 unbaked store-bought or homemade 9″ (23 cm)-diameter piecrusts

MINT FUDGE PIE FILLING

2 C (12 oz) semisweet chocolate chips

2 C (12 oz) milk chocolate chips

1 tbsp (14 g) butter

1 (14 oz) can sweetened condensed milk

½ tsp vanilla extract

1 tsp mint extract

VANILLA-MINT GLAZE

1 ½ C (195 g) confectioners' sugar

2 tbsp (29 ml) milk or water

¼ tsp vanilla extract

1 tsp mint extract

1 to 2 drops green food coloring

1 large egg white, beaten, for brushing

1 (3 oz [84 g]) bottle white nonpareils

Preheat the oven to 375°F (190°C).

Grease an 8-inch (20 cm) square baking pan, and grease and flour a large baking sheet.

To prepare the filling: In a double boiler over medium heat, combine the chocolate chips, butter and condensed milk and stir until melted and smooth. Add in the extracts and stir until well blended.

Pour mixture into the greased pan and let cool to room temperature. Refrigerate until set. Cut into small portions to use for the pie pop filling right away.

To prepare the glaze: Mix the confectioners' sugar, milk or water, vanilla and mint extracts together until creamy. If the glaze is too runny, add more sugar; if it is too thick, add more water ½ tsp at a time.

Once the glaze has the right consistency, add the green food coloring 1 drop at a time, mixing thoroughly before adding more, until you get the desired hue.

To assemble the pie pops: Flour both sides of the two piecrusts, then roll flat with a rolling pin. Using a 3-inch (7.6 cm) round cookie cutter, cut twenty-four rounds from the dough, twelve for the bottom crust and twelve for the top crust.

Lay out the twelve bottom crusts on the prepared baking sheet. Brush each bottom crust with egg white, using a silicone basting brush. Press an 8-inch (20 cm)-long cookie stick firmly on top of the center of each bottom crust. Place a 2-inch (5 cm)-square piece of fudge in the center of each bottom crust, taking care not to make the fudge too bulky (as it will melt and expand once baked). Place a top crust over each bottom crust and press firmly around the sides only, sealing the filling inside.

Create a cookie stick dowel by cutting a 1-inch (2.5 cm)-long piece off the end of an 8-inch (20 cm)-long cookie stick. Use this dowel to crimp the sealed edges of the pie pop by pressing firmly on each side of the stick first, then move counterclockwise around the edges. This will keep the stick from moving around once the pie pop is baked.

After each pop is sealed and pressed, brush more egg white on each top crust.

Bake the sheet on the center rack of the oven for 15 to 18 minutes, until the crust is nice and golden. Then place the individual pops on a cooling rack. While they are still warm, brush each pop with the glaze and sprinkle the white nonpareils on top; let the glaze set before moving. Allow to dry completely before handling.

Nutella S'more

The campfire, the camping chairs, stars in the night sky . . . and s'mores—that's how I remember our summer camping trips as a kid growing up in Middle America. With such simple ingredients, this pop isn't complicated and the Nutella adds that toasted nutty flavor to the chocolate that's sure to be a hit among classic s'more fans. These little pie pops package everything you love about this campfire goody into one neat little morsel.

YIELD: 2 DOZEN PIE POPS

---

1 recipe Homemade Pie Pop Crust (page 13), or 4 unbaked store-bought or homemade 9" (23 cm)-diameter piecrusts

MARSHMALLOW FLUFF FILLING

¾ C (143 g) granulated sugar

½ C (118 ml) light corn syrup

¼ C (59 ml) water

⅛ tsp fine salt

2 large egg whites, at room temperature

¼ tsp cream of tartar

1 ½ tsp vanilla extract

VANILLA GLAZE

1 tsp butter

1 ½ C (195 g) confectioners' sugar

2 tbsp (29 ml) milk or water

¼ tsp vanilla extract

1 (13 oz [371 g]) jar Nutella

1 large egg, beaten, for brushing

½ C (64 g) graham cracker crumbles

Preheat the oven to 375°F (190°C). Grease and flour a large baking sheet.

To prepare the filling: Stir together the granulated sugar, corn syrup, water and salt in a small saucepan over high heat. Bring to a boil, stirring occasionally, until the mixture reaches 240°F (115°C) on a candy thermometer.

In a large mixing bowl, beat the egg whites and cream of tartar with an electric mixer on medium speed, until soft peaks form. (You will want your egg whites whipped and ready for the sugar syrup to be drizzled in. If they are whipping faster than the sugar syrup is coming to temperature, stop whipping until the sugar mixture is ready).

When the syrup and egg whites are both ready, slowly drizzle 2 tablespoons (29 ml) of sugar syrup into the egg whites (don't add to much or the eggs will scramble). Slowly drizzle in the rest of the syrup. Begin beating the eggs with the syrup on medium-high speed and whip until stiff and glossy (5 to 7 minutes). Add the vanilla and whip for another 2 minutes.

To prepare the glaze: Melt the butter, then add all the other ingredients. Stir until creamy. If the glaze is too runny, add more sugar; if it is too thick, add more water ½ tsp at a time.

To assemble the pie pops: Flour both sides of the two piecrusts, then roll flat with a rolling pin. Using a 3-inch (7.6 cm) round cookie cutter, cut twenty-four rounds from the dough, twelve for the bottom crust and twelve for the top crust.

Lay out the twelve bottom crusts on the prepared baking sheet. Brush each bottom crust with egg white, using a silicone basting brush. Press an 8-inch (20 cm)-long cookie stick firmly on top of the center of each bottom crust.

(continued)

Dispense a 1 ½-inch (about 4 cm) dollop of marshmallow fluff mixed with Nutella in the center of each bottom crust. Place a top crust over each bottom crust and press firmly around the sides only, sealing the filling inside. Be careful not to overfill as the marshmallow will expand while baking.

Create a cookie stick dowel by cutting a 1-inch (2.5 cm)-long piece off the end of an 8-inch (20 cm)-long cookie stick. Use this dowel to crimp the sealed edges of the pie pop by pressing firmly on each side of the stick first, then move counterclockwise around the edges. This will keep the stick from moving around once the pie pop is baked.

After each pop is sealed and pressed, brush more egg white on each top crust.

Bake the sheet on the center rack of the oven for 15 to 18 minutes, until the crust is nice and golden. Then place the individual pops on a cooling rack. While they are still warm, brush each pop with the glaze and sprinkle with graham cracker crumbles; let the glaze set before moving. Allow to dry completely before handling.

Perfectly Pumpkin

Is there anything more homey than a good pumpkin pie? One of my favorite poems my grandfather used to read to me was "When the Frost in on the Punkin" by James Whitcomb Riley. It's a wonderful literary illustration of the beauty of fall; and nothing signals fall like pumpkins! Perfectly Pumpkin pie pops are a staple of the cooling weather, turning leaves and baking treats in our house. They are simple but oh-so-perfectly yummy.

YIELD: 2 DOZEN PIE POPS

---

1 recipe Homemade Pie Pop Crust (page 13), or 4 unbaked store-bought or homemade 9" (23 cm)-diameter piecrusts

PUMPKIN PIE FILLING
¾ C (143 g) granulated sugar

1 tsp ground cinnamon

½ tsp salt

½ tsp ground ginger

¼ tsp ground cloves

2 large eggs

1 (15 oz [425 g]) can pure pumpkin puree

1 (12 oz [412 ml]) evaporated milk

1 large egg white, beaten, for brushing

1:1 mixture of coarse sugar and ground cinnamon, for garnish

Preheat the oven to 450°F (232°C). Grease and flour a large baking sheet.

To prepare the filling: In a small bowl, mix together the granulated sugar, cinnamon, salt, ginger and cloves. In a larger bowl, beat the eggs until slightly foamy. Add the pumpkin puree to the eggs and then add the sugar mixture. Stir together. Gradually stir in the evaporated milk.

Pour into a 9-inch (23 cm)-diameter deep pie dish. Bake for 15 minutes, then lower the heat to 350°F (176°C) and bake for 45 to 50 minutes, or until a knife inserted into the center comes out clean. Increase oven temperature to 375°F (190°C).

To assemble the pie pops: Flour both sides of the two piecrusts, then roll flat with a rolling pin. Using a 3-inch (7.6 cm) round cookie cutter, cut twenty-four rounds, twelve for the bottom crust and twelve for the top crust.

Lay out the twelve bottom crusts on the prepared baking sheet. Brush each bottom crust with egg white, using a silicone basting brush. Press an 8-inch (20 cm)-long cookie stick firmly on top of the center of each bottom crust.

Dispense a 1 ½-inch (about 4 cm) dollop of pumpkin pie filling in the center of each bottom crust. Place a top crust over each bottom crust and press firmly around the sides only, sealing the filling inside.

Create a cookie stick dowel by cutting a 1-inch (2.5 cm)-long piece off the end of an 8-inch (20 cm)-long cookie stick. Use this dowel to crimp the sealed edges of the pie pop by pressing firmly on each side of the stick first, then move counterclockwise around the edges. This will keep the stick from moving around once the pie pop is baked. After each pop is sealed and pressed, brush more egg white on each top crust and sprinkle with the cinnamon sugar.

Bake the sheet on the center rack of the oven for 15 to 18 minutes, until the crust is nice and golden. Then place the individual pops on a cooling rack and let cool for at least 15 minutes before serving.

Honeyed Fig

I love a chilled glass of Chardonnay or Riesling in the late summer, and one of my favorite pairings for an *amuse-bouche* would be honeyed figs and cheese . . . simply to die for. I know that figs are typically suited for tarts rather than pies, so I wanted to make sure the crust was sweet enough to pass the test. Even if figs were not your cup of tea before, they will be now.

YIELD: 2 DOZEN PIE POPS

---

1 recipe Homemade Pie Pop Crust (page 13), or 4 unbaked store-bought or homemade 9″ (23 cm)-diameter piecrusts

FIG & CHEESE FILLING
½ C (120 g) cream cheese, softened
½ C (118 ml) whipping cream
1 large egg
½ C (100 g) brown sugar
¼ C (24 g) all-purpose flour
¼ tsp salt
¼ C (85 g) honey
5 C (828 g) brown or black figs, chopped small

Olive oil, for garnish
Fresh rosemary, for garnish

Preheat the oven to 350°F (176°C). Grease and flour a large baking sheet.

To prepare the filling: In a large bowl, mix together the cream cheese, cream, egg, brown sugar, flour, salt and honey. Toss in the chopped figs and stir.

Pour into a 9-inch (23 cm)-diameter pie dish. Bake for 20 to 25 minutes. Allow to cool to room temperature before using in pie pops. Increase oven temperature to 375°F (190°C).

To assemble the pie pops: Flour both sides of the two piecrusts, then roll flat with a rolling pin. Using a 3-inch (7.6 cm) round cookie cutter, cut out twenty-four rounds from the dough, twelve for the bottom crust and twelve for the top crust.

Lay out the twelve bottom crusts on the prepared baking sheet. Brush each bottom crust with egg white, using a silicone basting brush. Press an 8-inch (20 cm)-long cookie stick firmly on top of the center of each bottom crust.

Dispense a 1 ½-inch (about 4 cm) dollop of fig mixture in the center of each bottom crust. Place a top crust over each bottom crust and press firmly around the sides only, sealing the filling inside.

Create a cookie stick dowel by cutting a 1-inch (2.5 cm)-long piece off the end of an 8-inch (20 cm)-long cookie stick. Use this dowel to crimp the sealed edges of the pie pop by pressing firmly on each side of the stick first, then move counterclockwise around the edges. This will keep the stick from moving around once the pie pop is baked.

After each pop is sealed and pressed, brush olive oil on each top crust and sprinkle with fresh rosemary.

Bake the sheet on the center rack of the oven for 15 to 18 minutes, until the crust is nice and golden. Then place the individual pops on a cooling rack and let cool for at least 15 minutes before serving.

Peanut Butter & Chocolate

Peanut butter and chocolate is perhaps my favorite combination of sweet and savory, and this pop is a top favorite among my customers. It's no secret that traditional peanut butter pie is pretty dense and can sit a little heavy after a heaping plateful. I wanted to make a bite-size portion that all PB&C lovers can enjoy without having to consider the indulgence a guilty pleasure. Enjoy it with a tall glass of ice-cold milk and you're set.

YIELD: 2 DOZEN PIE POPS

1 recipe Homemade Pie Pop Crust (page 13), or 4 unbaked store-bought or homemade 9" (23 cm)-diameter piecrusts

PEANUT BUTTER FILLING

1 C (191 g) sugar

½ C (118 ml) milk

½ C (90 g) smooth peanut butter

8 oz (226 g) cream cheese, softened

1 large egg white, beaten, for brushing

½ C (64 g) crumbled chocolate graham crackers, for garnish

Preheat the oven to 375°F (190°C). Grease and flour a large baking sheet.

To prepare the filling: Combine the sugar and milk in a medium-size bowl and stir until the sugar is slightly dissolved. Add the peanut butter and cream cheese and stir until well blended. Use for pie pop filling right away.

To assemble the pie pops: Flour both sides of the two piecrusts, then roll flat with a rolling pin. Using a 3-inch (7.6 cm) round cookie cutter, cut twenty-four rounds from the dough, twelve for the bottom crust and twelve for the top crust.

Lay out the twelve bottom crusts on a large, greased and floured baking sheet. Brush each bottom crust with egg white, using a silicone basting brush. Press an 8-inch (20 cm)-long cookie stick firmly on top of the center of each bottom crust.

Dispense a 1 ½-inch (about 4 cm) dollop of peanut butter mixture in the center of each bottom crust. Place a top crust over each bottom crust and press firmly around the sides only, sealing the filling inside.

Create a cookie stick dowel by cutting a 1-inch (2.5 cm)-long piece off the end of an 8-inch (20 cm)-long cookie stick. Use this dowel to crimp the sealed edges of the pie pop by pressing firmly on each side of the stick first, then move counterclockwise around the edges. This will keep the stick from moving around once the pie pop is baked.

After each pop is sealed and pressed, brush more egg white on each top crust, and while wet, sprinkle with chocolate graham cracker crumbles.

Bake the sheet on the center rack of the oven for 15 to 18 minutes, until the crust is nice and golden. Then place the individual pops on a cooling rack and let cool for at least 15 minutes before serving.

3

Scrumptious & Savory Pie Pops

I'm sure it goes without saying that I love sweets. However, I definitely have what I call a "savory tooth." I love salt, cheese, spices . . . and I love them even more in pie form. Or, better yet, pie *pop* form. I'm not saying I invented the wheel when it comes to this idea; chicken pot pies and quiches are well-known and classic home-style favorites. Yet presenting them as pie pops keeps these flavor combos fresh and new. I also have quite a few original recipes that you will come to love just as much.

These are my most recent additions to my menu, and in many ways, were the most fun of all my recipes to create. I tried thinking of flavor profiles that I loved to pair with wine, appetizers, or even as an entrée. Savory pops open up an even wider realm of possibilities for using these treats for your dinner or party. You now have pie pop choices for a party celebrated at any hour of the day!

Breakfast Casserole

Breakfast is by far my most-loved meal! I believe it sets the mood for the whole day, so you'd better make it good! Not everyone is a breakfast fan, but these egg, sausage and cheese pops are perfect for convincing anyone. This particular casserole is a family favorite from my mother's kitchen. I find these pops work well with any breakfast or brunch and definitely add some fun to the standard morning menu. These pops are pretty, savory and mighty tasty.

YIELD: 2 DOZEN PIE POPS

1 recipe Homemade Pie Pop Crust (page 13), or 4 unbaked store-bought or homemade 9" (23 cm)-diameter piecrusts

CASEROLE FILLING

4 large eggs, beaten

1 C (236 ml) milk

½ tsp salt

½ tsp freshly ground black pepper

1 C (120 g) shredded sharp Cheddar cheese

½ lb (226 g) spicy pork sausage, browned and drained

3 slices of bread, torn into 1" (2.5 cm) pieces

1 large egg, beaten, for brushing

1:3 mixture of sea salt and freshly ground black pepper, for garnish

Preheat the oven to 350°F (176°C). Grease an 8-inch (20 cm) square baking pan, and grease and flour a large baking sheet.

To prepare the filling: In a large bowl, combine the eggs, milk, salt and pepper. Add shredded cheese and sausage. Last, add the torn pieces of bread and stir everything together by hand.

Pour into the prepared baking pan and bake for 30 to 40 minutes, until set and slightly browned. Cut into small portions to use for the pie pop filling right away. Increase the oven temperature to 375°F (190°C).

To assemble the pie pops: Flour both sides of the two piecrusts, then roll flat with a rolling pin. Using a 3-inch (7.6 cm) round cookie cutter, cut twenty-four rounds from the dough, twelve for the bottom crust and twelve for the top crust.

Lay out the twelve bottom crusts on the prepared baking sheet. Brush each bottom crust with egg white, using a silicone basting brush. Press an 8-inch (20 cm)-long cookie stick firmly on top of the center of each bottom crust.

Dispense a 1 ½-inch (about 4 cm) piece of casserole filling in the center of each bottom crust. Place a top crust over each bottom crust and press firmly around the sides only, sealing the filling inside.

(continued)

Create a cookie stick dowel by cutting a 1-inch (2.5 cm)-long piece off the end of an 8-inch (20 cm)-long cookie stick. Use this dowel to crimp the sealed edges of the pie pop by pressing firmly on each side of the stick first, then move counterclockwise around the edges. This will keep the stick from moving around once the pie pop is baked.

After each pop is sealed and pressed, brush more egg white on each top crust. Finally, sprinkle top crusts with the garnish mixture of salt and pepper.

Bake the sheet on the center rack of the oven for 15 to 18 minutes, until the crust is nice and golden. Then place the individual pops on a cooling rack and let cool for at least 15 minutes before serving.

Hot Ham & Cheese

Inspired by one of my favorite quick-dinner sandwiches that my mother would always make on hectic weeknights, Hot Ham & Cheese is another great option for a savory pie. The bitter mustard and ham pair wonderfully with the salty Swiss cheese and subtle crunch of the poppy seeds. Once a favorite, always a favorite.

YIELD: 2 DOZEN PIE POPS

1 recipe Homemade Pie Pop Crust (page 13), or 4 unbaked store-bought or homemade 9" (23 cm)-diameter piecrusts

HOT HAM & CHEESE FILLING

¼ C (229 g) butter, at room temperature

3 tbsp (28 g) chopped yellow onion

3 tbsp (47 g) Dijon mustard

1 tbsp (8 g) poppy seeds

8 oz (226 g) Swiss cheese, shredded

8 oz (226 g) cooked ham, chopped

1 large egg, beaten, for brushing

Parmesan cheese (shredded or crumbled), for garnish

Olive oil, for garnish

Poppy seeds, for garnish

Preheat the oven to 375°F (190°C). Grease and flour a large baking sheet.

To prepare the filling: Combine the butter and onion in a saucepan and cook over medium-low heat until the onion is slightly cooked. Add the mustard and poppy seeds. Remove from the heat and allow to cool.

To assemble the pie pops: Flour both sides of the two piecrusts, then roll flat with a rolling pin. Using a 3-inch (7.6 cm) round cookie cutter, cut twenty-four rounds from the dough, twelve for the bottom crust and twelve for the top crust.

Lay out the twelve bottom crusts on the prepared baking sheet. Brush each bottom crust with egg white, using a silicone basting brush. Press an 8-inch (20 cm)-long cookie stick firmly on top of the center of each bottom crust.

Dispense a 1 ½-inch (about 4 cm) dollop of mustard sauce in the center of each bottom crust, spreading the filling outward to the edges. Then sprinkle with shredded cheese and top with two or three pieces of chopped ham. Place a top crust over each bottom crust and press firmly around the sides only, sealing the filling inside.

Create a cookie stick dowel by cutting a 1-inch (2.5 cm)-long piece off the end of an 8-inch (20 cm)-long cookie stick. Use this dowel to crimp the sealed edges of the pie pop by pressing firmly on each side of the stick first, then move counterclockwise around the edges. This will keep the stick from moving around once the pie pop is baked.

After each pop is sealed and pressed, brush olive oil on each top crust and sprinkle with Parmesan cheese and poppy seeds.

Bake the sheet on the center rack of the oven for 15 to 18 minutes until the crust is nice and golden. Then place the individual pops on a cooling rack and let cool for at least 15 minutes before serving.

Pizza Pocket

Pizza. Is there any other food that is so versatile, so yummy and beloved by all? There are so many ways to prepare and enjoy pizza, the flavor combinations are endless. So, while this variation of a pizza pocket will be kept simple, don't be afraid to add toppings that you enjoy. Any will work. For the kiddos, and simplicity's sake, we're doing a traditional pepperoni pizza pocket pie pop, complete with a Parmesan crust!

YIELD: 2 DOZEN PIE POPS

1 recipe Homemade Pie Pop Crust (page 13), or 4 unbaked store-bought or homemade 9" (23 cm)-diameter piecrusts

PIZZA PIE FILLING

4 garlic cloves, minced

1 14 oz (414 ml) can marinara sauce or pizza sauce

1 large egg, beaten, for brushing

1 C (120 g) shredded fresh mozzarella or provolone cheese

½ C (90 g) chopped (into small pieces) chorizo or pepperoni

3 oz (85 g) fresh basil leaves, chopped, or 1 oz (28 g) dried

Olive oil, for garnish

Garlic salt, for garnish

Parmesan cheese, shredded or crumbled, for garnish

Preheat the oven to 375°F (190°C). Grease and flour a large baking sheet.

To assemble the pie pops: Stir the garlic into the marinara sauce and set aside.

Flour both sides of the two piecrusts, then roll flat with a rolling pin. Using a 3-inch (7.6 cm) round cookie cutter, cut twenty-four rounds from the dough, twelve for the bottom crust and twelve for the top crust.

Lay out the twelve bottom crusts on the prepared baking sheet. Brush each bottom crust with egg white, using a silicone basting brush. Press an 8-inch (20 cm)-long cookie stick firmly on top of the center of each bottom crust.

Dispense a 1 ½-inch (about 4 cm) dollop of marinara sauce mixture in the center of each bottom crust, spreading the filling outward to the edges. Then sprinkle with the shredded cheese, and finally top with the chorizo and basil. Place a top crust over each bottom crust and press firmly around the sides only, sealing the filling inside.

Create a cookie stick dowel by cutting a 1-inch (2.5 cm)-long piece off the end of an 8-inch (20 cm)-long cookie stick. Use this dowel to crimp the sealed edges of the pie pop by pressing firmly on each side of the stick first, then move counterclockwise around the edges. This will keep the stick from moving around once the pie pop is baked.

After each pop is sealed and pressed, brush olive oil on each crust and sprinkle with garlic salt and Parmesan cheese.

Bake the sheet on the center rack of the oven for 15 to 18 minutes, until the crust is nice and golden. Then place the individual pops on a cooling rack and let cool for at least 15 minutes before serving.

Sweet Potato

Sweet potatoes are naturally sweet, of course, and therefore this little root vegetable commonly tells my taste buds, "Dessert!" A little sugar, vanilla and a pinch of cinnamon and nutmeg are really all you need to bring this pop to full flavor. Introduce Sweet Potato pie pops at your family affair and they are sure to become a new holiday tradition.

YIELD: 2 DOZEN PIE POPS

1 recipe Homemade Pie Pop Crust (page 13), or 4 unbaked store-bought or homemade 9" (23 cm)-diameter piecrusts

SWEET POTATO FILLING

1 lb (453 g) sweet potatoes

½ C (229 g) butter, at room temperature

1 C (191 g) granulated sugar

½ C (118 ml) milk

2 large eggs

½ tsp ground nutmeg

½ tsp ground cinnamon

1 tsp vanilla extract

1 large egg, beaten, for brushing

1:1 mixture of coarse sugar and ground cinnamon, for garnish

Pecan halves, for garnish

Preheat the oven to 350°F (176°C). Grease and flour a large baking sheet.

To prepare the filling: Boil the sweet potatoes whole in their skins for 40 to 50 minutes, or until done. Run cold water over the potatoes and remove the skins. Break apart the potatoes in a large bowl, adding the butter; mix well with an electric mixer at low speed.

Stir in the granulated sugar, milk, eggs, nutmeg, cinnamon and vanilla. Beat on medium speed until the mixture is smooth.

Pour the filling into a 9-inch (23 cm)-diameter pie dish. Bake for 55 to 60 minutes, until a knife inserted into the center comes out clean. (The pie will sink some as it cools.) Let cool to room temperature. Increase the oven temperature to 375°F (190°C).

To assemble the pie pops: Flour both sides of the two piecrusts, then roll flat with a rolling pin. Using a 3-inch (7.6 cm) round cookie cutter, cut twenty-four rounds from the dough, twelve for the bottom crust and twelve for the top crust.

Lay out the twelve bottom crusts on a large, greased and floured baking sheet. Brush each bottom crust with egg white, using a silicone basting brush. Press an 8-inch (20 cm)-long cookie stick firmly on top of the center of each bottom crust.

Dispense a 1 ½-inch (about 4 cm) dollop of sweet potato filling in the center of each bottom crust. Place a top crust over each bottom crust and press firmly around the sides only, sealing the filling inside.

Create a cookie stick dowel by cutting a 1-inch (2.5 cm)-long piece off the end of an 8-inch (20 cm)-long cookie stick. Use this dowel to crimp the sealed edges of the pie pop by pressing firmly on each side of the stick first, then move counterclockwise around the edges. This will keep the stick from moving around once the pie pop is baked.

After each pop is sealed and pressed, sprinkle each top crust with the cinnamon sugar and place one pecan half in the center.

Bake the sheet on the center rack of the oven for 15 to 18 minutes, until the crust is nice and golden. Then place the individual pops on a cooling rack and let cool for at least 15 minutes before serving.

Gouda-Broccoli Quiche

Quiches and frittatas are some of the dishes that make for a great breakfast, lunch or dinner . . . or in this case, pie pop! This recipe works well for any party set at any time of day.

YIELD 2 DOZEN PIE POPS

1 recipe Homemade Pie Pop Crust (page 13), or 4 unbaked store-bought or homemade 9″ (23 cm)-diameter piecrusts

QUICHE FILLING

2 C (681 g) fresh or frozen broccoli florets

4 large eggs

1 C (236 ml) half-and-half

1 C (120 g) smoked Gouda, shredded

½ tsp sea salt

¼ tsp garlic powder

⅛ tsp ground nutmeg

⅛ tsp freshly ground white pepper

3 strips bacon, fried and crumbled

1 large egg, beaten, for brushing

Freshly ground white or black pepper, for garnish

Preheat the oven to 350°F (176°C). Grease and flour a large baking sheet.

To prepare the filling: Blanch the broccoli, or if you are using frozen, thaw completely. Beat together the eggs and half-and-half; add the shredded cheese and mix well. Stir in the broccoli, salt, garlic powder, nutmeg and pepper. Last, add the cooked bacon crumbles.

Pour into a 9-inch (23 cm)-diameter pie dish and bake for 30 to 35 minutes, or until a knife inserted into the center comes out clean. Cut into small portions to use for the pie pop filling right away. Increase oven temperature to 375°F (190°C).

To assemble the pie pops: Flour both sides of the two piecrusts, then roll flat with a rolling pin. Using a 3-inch (7.6 cm) round cookie cutter, cut twenty-four rounds, twelve for the bottom crust and twelve for the top crust.

Lay out the twelve bottom crusts on the prepared baking sheet. Brush each bottom crust with egg white, using a silicone basting brush. Press an 8-inch (20 cm)-long cookie stick firmly on top of the center of each bottom crust.

Place a 1-½ inch (about 4 cm) square piece of quiche in the center of each bottom crust. Place a top crust over each bottom crust and press firmly around the sides only, sealing the filling inside.

Create a cookie stick dowel by cutting a 1-inch (2.5 cm)-long piece off the end of an 8-inch (20 cm)-long cookie stick. Use this dowel to crimp the sealed edges of the pie pop by pressing firmly on each side of the stick first, then move counterclockwise around the edges. This will keep the stick from moving around once the pie pop is baked.

After each pop is sealed and pressed, brush more egg white on each top crust and sprinkle with ground pepper.

Bake the sheet on the center rack of the oven for 15 to 18 minutes, until the crust is nice and golden. Then place the individual pops on a cooling rack and let cool for at least 15 minutes before serving.

Chicken Pot Pie

Warm pot pies on a cold day are the ultimate comfort food. If you use fresh vegetables, organic chicken and 1% milk, you can cut down on calories yet still enjoy all the flavor you expect from this savory pie. Perfectly portioning this yummy creation into pie pops definitely makes you feel less guilty about going for seconds.

YIELD 2 DOZEN PIE POPS

1 recipe Homemade Pie Pop Crust (page 13), or 4 unbaked store-bought or homemade 9" (23 cm)-diameter piecrusts

CHICKEN POT PIE FILLING

1 lb (453 g) skinless, boneless chicken breast, cut into small cubes

1 C (229 g) sliced baby carrots

1 C (340 g) frozen green peas

½ C (114 g) sliced or chopped celery

⅓ C (50 g) chopped yellow onion

⅓ C (76 g) butter

⅓ C (33 g) all-purpose flour

½ tsp salt

¼ tsp freshly ground black pepper

½ tsp dried basil

½ tsp Season All salt

1 ¾ C (414 ml) chicken stock

⅔ C (157 ml) milk

1 large egg white, beaten, as for brushing

Preheat the oven to 425°F (218°C). Grease and flour a large baking sheet.

To prepare the filling: In a large saucepan, combine the chicken, carrots, peas and celery. Add water to cover, bring to a boil, then boil for 15 minutes. Remove from the heat and drain, then set aside.

In the same saucepan, sauté the onions in the butter over medium heat until soft. Stir in the flour, salt, pepper, basil and Season-All salt. Slowly stir in the chicken stock and milk. Simmer over medium-low heat until thick. On low heat, add the chicken and vegetables and stir, for another 5 to 10 minutes. Let cool to room temperature before using. Reduce oven temperature to 375°F (190°C).

To assemble the pie pops: Flour both sides of the two piecrusts, then roll flat with a rolling pin. Using a 3-inch (7.6 cm) round cookie cutter, cut twenty-four rounds, twelve for the bottom crust and twelve for the top crust. Lay out the twelve bottom crusts on the prepared baking sheet. Press an 8-inch (20 cm)-long cookie stick firmly on top of the center of each bottom crust.

Place a half-dollar sized amount of chicken pot pie mixture in the center of each bottom crust (make sure you include both chicken and veggies for each pop). Place a top crust over each bottom crust and press firmly around the sides only, sealing the filling inside.

Create a cookie stick dowel by cutting a 1-inch (2.5 cm)-long piece off the end of an 8-inch (20 cm)-long cookie stick. Use this dowel to crimp the sealed edges of the pie pop by pressing firmly on each side of the stick first, then move counterclockwise around the edges. This will keep the stick from moving around once the pie pop is baked.

After each pop is sealed and pressed, brush egg white on each top crust.

Bake the sheet on the center rack of the oven for 15 to 18 minutes, until the crust is nice and golden. Then place the individual pops on a cooling rack and let cool for at least 15 minutes before serving.

Vegetable Roll

One of my favorite variations on the classic egg roll is to bake rather than deep fry them! I find it seals in the flavors just as well, and of course, it is much healthier, too. The filling of this Chinese-American appetizer features crisp veggies and salty soy sauce and ginger. It bakes well inside the pastry, which could very soon take over the traditional egg roll wrappers as our favorite way to enjoy these little rolls.

YIELD: 2 DOZEN PIE POPS

1 recipe Homemade Pie Pop Crust (page 13), or 4 unbaked store-bought or homemade 9″ (23 cm)-diameter piecrusts

VEGETABLE ROLL FILLING

1 tsp olive oil

2 C (681 g) chopped savoy cabbage

2 C (681 g) shredded carrots

2 C (99 g) bean sprouts

1 (5 oz [141 g]) can water chestnuts, drained and chopped

1 tsp ground ginger

¼ tsp salt

1 tbsp (9 g) cornstarch

¼ C (59 ml) water

2 tbsp (29 ml) soy sauce

2 tbsp (6 g) sliced green onion or scallion

1 large egg white, beaten, for brushing

Olive oil, for garnish

Preheat the oven to 375°F (190°C). Grease and flour a large baking sheet.

To prepare the filling: Heat the olive oil in a large skillet over medium heat. Once hot, add the cabbage, carrots, sprouts, water chestnuts, ginger and salt to the pan and cook, stirring frequently, for 4 to 5 minutes (the vegetables should be heated through but still be slightly crisp).

Mix the cornstarch with the water and blend thoroughly. Add the cornstarch mixture and the soy sauce to the pan, along with the green onions. Cook for an additional 1 to 2 minutes, or until the sauce thickens. Remove from the heat and let cool for 15 minutes, until no longer steaming; use for pie pops right away.

To assemble the pie pops: Flour both sides of the two piecrusts, then roll flat with a rolling pin. Using a 3-inch (7.6 cm) round cookie cutter, cut twenty-four rounds from the dough, twelve for the bottom crust and twelve for the top crust.

Lay out the twelve bottom crusts on the prepared baking sheet. Brush each bottom crust with egg white, using a silicone basting brush. Press an 8-inch (20 cm)-long cookie stick firmly on top of the center of each bottom crust.

Place a half-dollar-sized amount of vegetable roll filling in the center of each bottom crust. Place a top crust over each bottom crust and press firmly around the sides only, sealing the filling inside.

Create a cookie stick dowel by cutting a 1-inch (2.5 cm)-long piece off the end of an 8-inch (20 cm)-long cookie stick. Use this dowel to crimp the sealed edges of the pie pop by pressing firmly on each side of the stick first, then move counterclockwise around the edges. This will keep the stick from moving around once the pie pop is baked.

After each pop is sealed and pressed, brush olive oil on each top crust.

Bake the sheet on the center rack of the oven for 15 to 18 minutes, until the crust is nice and golden. Then place the individual pops on a cooling rack and let cool for at least 15 minutes before serving.

4

Cake Pops—A Piece of Cake

Cake pops hit the culinary scene several years ago. As the first mini dessert I ever offered they will always hold a special place in my heart. They are super moist, decadent and melt-in-your-mouth marvelous!

These recipes follow the original method of making cake pops, which is to incorporate crumbled sheet cake and cream cheese or buttercream frosting into a ready-to-eat "dough." The cake balls are then dipped into melted candy melts or chocolate and garnished with sprinkles or other toppings. This is by far the best way to keep your cake pops moist (especially if you're not planning on eating them right away), and in my opinion, the tastiest, too.

Cake pops are always a huge hit at parties and seem to be overtaking the vastly popular cupcake. Just like my pie pops, they are so colorful and easily customized, they fit into any decor or theme.

TIME-SAVING TIPS

- If you have one to two days to work with, make the cake(s) ahead of time. You can bake the cakes and form them into the cake pop dough up to one week ahead of time. Just be sure to refrigerate the dough in an airtight container.
- If you are making more than three dozen cake pops, roll the cake balls one to two days ahead of time. Refrigerate them in an airtight container (do not freeze) for optimal freshness.
- Cake pops will last for about five days. They will still taste great as long as you prepare and execute them as specified in this section. Keep them out of direct sunlight and in a cool/room-temperature environment. **Tip: Do not refrigerate them after completed because this can cause condensation to build up on the outer candy shell.**

Lemon Poppy Seed

Lemon is definitely my go-to citrus fruit for adding conventional flavor, and a little goes a long way. People are always surprised at how little lemon zest you need to really pull out that strong foundation that makes my Lemon Poppy Seed cake pops so intriguing. The Lemon Cream Cheese Frosting does give it that extra push of flavor for lemon fans, but try a standard buttercream frosting if you are looking for a more subtle addition. Either way, this pop is always a favorite among cake pop connoisseurs.

YIELD: *2 DOZEN CAKE POPS*

LEMON POPPY SEED CAKE

2 ¼ C (202 g) cake flour

1 ⅛ C (215 g) granulated sugar

1 tsp salt

1 ½ tbsp (14 g) lemon zest

4 ½ tbsp (38 g) poppy seeds

1 ⅓ C (306 g) unsalted butter, at room temperature

5 large eggs

2 tsp vanilla extract

LEMON CREAM CHEESE FROSTING

Makes about 3 ⅔ cups (457 g) frosting

1 (8 oz [226 g]) package cream cheese, softened

¼ C (57 g) butter, at room temperature

2 tbsp (29 ml) freshly squeezed lemon juice

2 tsp lemon zest

1 tsp vanilla extract

5 C (650 g) confectioners' sugar

1 (12 oz [340 g]) bag yellow candy melts

1 (12 oz [340 g]) bag white candy melts

Preheat the oven to 350°F (204°C). Grease and flour a 9 x 5-inch (22 x 12 cm) loaf pan.

To prepare the cake: In a medium-size bowl, sift together the flour, granulated sugar and salt. Mix in the lemon zest, poppy seeds and butter. Add the eggs, one at a time, beating well after each addition. Add the vanilla.

Pour the batter into the prepared loaf pan and bake for 1 hour and 15 minutes (if necessary, cover the top with foil toward the end of baking so the top does not brown), until a toothpick inserted into the center of the loaf comes out clean. Remove from the oven and let cool until no longer warm to the touch.

To prepare the frosting: In a large bowl, beat the cream cheese, butter, lemon juice, lemon zest and vanilla together until smooth and fluffy. Add the confectioners' sugar in two additions. Beat until creamy, adding more sugar or lemon juice, if needed, for a slightly thick consistency.

To prepare the candy melts: Heat half of the yellow candy melts in an electric melter, stirring occasionally, until smooth. Add the remaining half of the bag and stir until smooth. Turn the melter setting to low and stir the candy melts occasionally until ready to use. Alternatively, if you don't have an electric melter, you can use your microwave set at 50 percent to melt the candy. In a microwave-safe bowl, heat in increments of 15 seconds, stirring between each heating until melted.

To assemble the cake pops: In a large bowl, break apart the entire cake in sections until you get fine crumbles (should resemble bread crumbs). Add the cream cheese frosting 1 to 2 tablespoons (14 to 28 g) at a time, blending well with a spatula after each addition. You will start to see "dough" forming. Stop adding the frosting once the cake dough is the consistency of Play-Doh: moist but not soggy. Start molding the dough into a large ball with your hands, picking out any dry pieces of cake as you form. Chill the dough for 1 to 2 hours, until firm.

(continued)

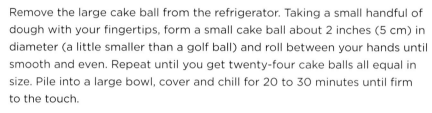

Remove the large cake ball from the refrigerator. Taking a small handful of dough with your fingertips, form a small cake ball about 2 inches (5 cm) in diameter (a little smaller than a golf ball) and roll between your hands until smooth and even. Repeat until you get twenty-four cake balls all equal in size. Pile into a large bowl, cover and chill for 20 to 30 minutes until firm to the touch.

Remove your cake balls from the refrigerator. Dip about ¾ inch (2 cm) of the end of a 6 inch (15 cm)-long candy stick into the melted yellow candy melts. While still hot, insert this end into the center of a cake ball and use your hand to secure and position the ball securely on the stick.

Dip the cake ball (now secured to the candy stick) back into the melted yellow candy melts and lightly twist the stick in a counterclockwise motion until the entire ball is completely covered.

Place the frosted cake pop into a Styrofoam brick or cake pop rack to let cool and dry. Repeat the above steps for all twenty-four cake pops.

In a separate electric melter, melt half of the white candy melts, stirring until smooth. Turn the heat setting to low and continue to heat the candy melts for about 15 minutes. Place the white melted candy into a disposable decorating bag with a #2 round tip.

Holding a cake pop horizontally by its stick, drizzle the melted candy over the frosted cake pop, using a side-to-side motion, gently squeezing the decorating bag with one hand while turning the cake pop with your other hand. Place the stick back in its Styrofoam holder and allow the drizzled candy melt coating to dry for at least 30 minutes before handling. Repeat until all twenty-four cake pops are decorated.

Couture Coconut

Coconuts are a wondrous little fruit (not actually a nut). The flesh, or copra, and the milk that is extracted from it are both extremely nutritious and very versatile for cooking and baking. Adding shredded coconut to the delicate white cake gives this cake pop a fantastic texture inside, while the additional coconut on top gives the pop a fun finishing touch that looks really couture.

YIELD: 2 DOZEN CAKE POPS

COCONUT CAKE

3 C (269 g) cake flour, sifted

2 tbsp (22 g) baking powder

¼ tsp salt

1 C (229 g) butter, at room temperature

16 oz (453 g) confectioners' sugar

4 large egg yolks, beaten

1 C (236 ml) whole milk

1 C (75 g) sweetened shredded coconut

2 tsp (10 ml) vanilla extract

1 tsp almond extract

4 large egg whites, beaten

CREAM CHEESE FROSTING

Makes about 3 ⅔ cups (457 g) frosting

1 (8 oz [226 g]) package cream cheese, softened

¼ C (57 g) butter, at room temperature

1 ½ tsp (7.4 ml) vanilla extract

2 C (260 g) confectioners' sugar, plus more if needed

1 (12 oz [340 g]) bag 340 g white candy melts

12 oz (340 g) sweetened shredded coconut, for garnish

Preheat the oven to 350°F (176°C). Grease and flour a 9 x 13-inch (22 x 33 cm) baking pan.

To prepare the cake: Sift the cake flour, baking powder and salt three times into a medium-size bowl.

In a separate large bowl, thoroughly cream the butter using an electric mixer at high speed, adding the confectioners' sugar gradually; continue creaming until light and fluffy.

Add the beaten egg yolks to the sugar mixture and beat well. Alternately add the flour mixture and milk to the butter mixture, beating well after each addition.

Stir in the coconut, vanilla and almond extract. Gently fold in the beaten egg whites.

Pour the batter into the prepared cake pan and bake for 30 to 35 minutes (if necessary, cover the top with foil toward the end of baking so the top does not brown), until a toothpick inserted into the center of the loaf comes out clean. Remove from the oven and let cool until no longer warm to the touch.

To prepare the frosting: In a large bowl, beat the cream cheese, butter and vanilla together with an electic mixer at medium speed, until smooth and fluffy. Add the confectioners' sugar in two additions. Beat until creamy, adding more sugar, if needed, for a slightly thick consistency.

To prepare the candy melts: Melt half of the white candy melts in an electric melter, stirring occasionally, until smooth. Add the remaining half of the bag and stir until smooth. Turn the melter setting to low and stir the candy melts occasionally until ready to use. Alternatively, if you don't have an electric melter, you can use your microwave set at 50 percent to melt the candy. In a microwave-safe bowl, heat in increments of 15 seconds, stirring between each heating until melted.

(continued)

To assemble the cake pops: In a large bowl, break apart the entire cake in sections until you get fine crumbles (should resemble bread crumbs). Add the cream cheese frosting 1 to 2 tablespoons (14 to 28 g) at a time, blending well with a spatula after each addition. You will start to see "dough" forming. Stop adding the frosting once the cake dough is the consistency of Play-Doh: moist but not soggy. Start molding the dough into a large bowl with your hands, picking out any dry pieces of cake as you form. Cover and chill the dough for 1 to 2 hours, until firm.

Remove your cake ball from the refrigerator. Taking a small handful of dough with your fingertips, form a small cake ball about 2 inches (5 cm) in diameter (a little smaller than a golf ball) and roll between your hands until smooth and even. Repeat until you get twenty-four cake balls all equal in size. Pile into a large bowl, cover and chill for 20 to 30 minutes, until firm to the touch.

Remove your cake balls from the refrigerator. Dip about ¾ inch (2 cm) of the end of a 6-inch (15 cm)-long candy stick into the melted white candy melts. While still hot, insert this end into the center of a cake ball and use your hand to secure and position the ball securely on the stick.

Dip the cake ball (now secured to the candy stick) back into the melted candy melts and lightly twist the stick in a counterclockwise motion until the entire ball is completely covered.

While the frosting is still wet, sprinkle the coconut on all sides of the cake pop. Place the frosted and decorated cake pop into a Styrofoam brick or cake pop rack to cool and dry. Repeat the above steps for all twenty-four cake pops.

Caramel Cacao

Originally I wanted to dip a chocolate cake ball into gooey caramel . . . but I quickly realized the mess was not always worth the effort. It was also impossible to package and ship these to my clients, as they would heat up and stick to their wrapping. Not that everyone would need to consider shipping when baking these pops; however, I want these to be easy to make, enjoy and share for any occasion near or far. I tried using caramel cake with dark chocolate candy coating topped with fresh sea salt. To my surprise, the reverse was not only good, but in my opinion, a pleasant twist on the beloved combination of chocolate and caramel.

YIELD: 2 DOZEN CAKE POPS

CARAMEL CAKE

2 C (198 g) all-purpose flour

1 tsp baking soda

1 tsp baking powder

½ tsp salt

¼ tsp ground cinnamon

½ C (114 g) unsalted butter, at room temperature

½ C (95) granulated sugar

½ C (100 g) brown sugar

2 large eggs

1 C (120 g) sour cream

1 tsp vanilla extract

CARAMEL FROSTING

Makes about 3 ⅔ cups (457 g) frosting

1 lb (453 g) confectioners' sugar

1 C (229 g) unsalted butter, at room temperature

2 C (402 g) light brown sugar, packed

¼ C (59 ml) whipping cream

1 tsp vanilla extract

1 (12 oz [340 g]) bag dark chocolate candy melts

Coarse sea salt, for garnish

Preheat the oven to 350°F (176°C). Grease and flour a 9 x 13-inch (22 x 33 cm) baking pan.

To prepare the cake: In a medium-size bowl, sift together flour, baking soda, baking powder, salt and cinnamon.

In a large bowl, cream together the butter, granulated sugar and brown sugar with an electric mixer on high speed until light and fluffy (about 5 minutes).

Beat in the eggs, one at a time, until well blended. Mix in the sour cream and vanilla at low speed until just incorporated. Beat in the flour mixture ½ cup (50 g) at a time on low speed, stirring and scraping after each addition.

Pour into the prepared baking pan and bake 40 to 50 minutes, or until a toothpick inserted into the center comes out clean. Remove from the oven and let cool until no longer warm to the touch.

To prepare the frosting: Sift the confectioners' sugar into a large bowl; set aside

In a heavy-bottomed saucepan, combine the butter and brown sugar and stir over medium-low heat until blended

Stir in the cream and bring the mixture to a full boil; immediately remove from the heat and add the vanilla. Set aside to cool until lukewarm.

Add the cream mixture to the confectioners' sugar and beat with an electric mixer on high speed until creamy and spreadable.

(continued

To prepare the candy melts: Heat half of the dark chocolate candy melts in an electric melter, stirring occasionally, until smooth. Add the remaining half of the bag and stir until smooth. Turn the melter setting to low and stir occasionally until ready to use. Alternatively, if you don't have an electric melter, you can use your microwave set at 50 percent to melt the candy. In a microwave-safe bowl, heat in increments of 15 seconds, stirring between each heating until melted.

To assemble the cake pops: In a large bowl, break apart the entire cake in sections until you get fine crumbles (should resemble bread crumbs). Add the caramel frosting 1 to 2 tablespoons (14 to 28 g) at a time, blending well with a spatula after each addition. You will start to see "dough" forming. Stop adding the frosting once the cake dough is the consistency of Play-Doh: moist but not soggy. Start molding the dough into a large ball with your hands, picking out any dry pieces of cake as you form. Cover and chill the dough for 1 to 2 hours, until firm.

Remove your cake ball from the refrigerator. Taking a small handful of dough with your fingertips, form a small cake ball about 2 inches (5 cm) in diameter (a little smaller than a golf ball) and roll between your hands until smooth and even. Repeat until you get twenty-four cake balls all equal in size. Pile into a large bowl, cover and chill for 20 to 30 minutes, until firm to the touch.

Remove your cake balls from the refrigerator. Dip about ¾ inch (2 cm) of the end of a 6-inch (15 cm)-long candy stick into the melted chocolate candy melts. While still hot, insert this end into the center of a cake ball and use your hand to secure and position the ball securely on the stick.

Dip the cake ball (now secured to the candy stick) back into the melted candy melts and lightly twist the stick in a counterclockwise motion until the entire ball is completely covered.

While the frosting is still wet, sprinkle coarse sea salt on top of the cake pop. Place the frosted and decorated cake pop into a Styrofoam brick or cake pop rack to let cool and dry. Repeat the above steps for all twenty-four cake pops.

Lavender-Honey

Recently, lavender has made a huge leap into the everyday kitchen, thanks to the trend of using naturals as a way to decorate culinary masterpieces. This wonderfully fragrant and edible little flower bud makes this cake pop all the more memorable. The sharp-sweet aroma of the dried bloom blends seamlessly with the butter and honey. Lavender has always reminded me of a country meadow in fading summer. It's not necessarily as familiar in flavor as say, vanilla or chocolate, but why play it safe all the time? These are a great way to get people talking . . . in a good way of course.

YIELD: 2 DOZEN CAKE POPS

LAVENDER-HONEY CAKE

1 ¾ (157 g) cake flour, sifted

1 ½ tsp (5.3 g) baking powder

½ tsp salt

2 tsp (1.3 g) dried culinary-grade lavender

½ C (114 g) butter, at room temperature

1 C (191 g) granulated sugar

¼ C (59 ml) honey

1 tsp vanilla extract

2 large eggs, at room temperature

⅔ C (157 ml) whole milk

CREAM CHEESE FROSTING

Makes about 3 ⅔ cup (457 g) frosting

1 (8 oz [226 g]) package cream cheese, softened

¼ C (57 g) butter, at room temperature

1 ½ tsp (7.4 g) vanilla extract

2 C (260 g) confectioners' sugar, plus more if needed

1 (12 oz [340 g]) bag lavender candy melts

8 oz (226 g) culinary-grade dried lavender, for garnish

Preheat the oven to 350°F (176°C). Grease and flour a 9 x 13-inch (22 x 33 cm) baking pan.

To prepare the cake: Sift cake flour, baking powder and salt three times into a medium-size bowl; add the lavender and set aside.

In a large mixing bowl, cream the butter thoroughly using an electric mixer at high speed, adding the granulated sugar, honey and vanilla and beating until well combined. Add the eggs, one at a time, beating well after each addition. Alternately add the flour mixture and the milk to the butter mixture, beating on low speed until just combined.

Pour the batter into the prepared cake pan and bake for 30 to 35 minutes (if necessary, cover the top with foil toward the end of baking so the top does not brown). Let cool until no longer warm to the touch.

To prepare the frosting: In a large bowl, beat the cream cheese, butter and vanilla together using an electric mixer at medium speed until smooth and fluffy. Add the confectioners' sugar in two additions. Beat until creamy, adding more sugar, if needed, for a slightly thick consistency.

To prepare the candy melts: Heat half of the lavender candy melts in an electric melter, stirring occasionally, until smooth. Add the remaining half of the bag and stir until smooth. Turn the melter setting to low and stir the candy melts occasionally until ready to use. Alternatively, if you don't have an electric melter, you can use your microwave set at 50 percent to melt the candy. In a microwave-safe bowl, heat in increments of 15 seconds, stirring between each heating until melted.

(continued)

To assemble the cake pops: In a large bowl, break apart the entire cake in sections until you get fine crumbles (should resemble bread crumbs). Add the cream cheese frosting 1 to 2 tablespoons (14 to 28 g) at a time, blending well with a spatula after each addition. You will start to see "dough" forming. Stop adding the frosting once the cake dough is the consistency of Play-Doh: moist but not soggy. Start molding the dough into a large bowl with your hands, picking out any dry pieces of cake as you form. Cover and chill the dough for 1 to 2 hours, until firm.

Remove the large cake ball from the refrigerator. Taking a small handful of dough with your fingertips, form a small cake ball about 2 inches (5 cm) in diameter (a little smaller than a golf ball) and roll between your hands until smooth and even. Repeat until you get twenty-four cake balls all equal in size. Pile into a large bowl, cover and chill for 20 to 30 minutes, until firm to the touch.

Remove your cake balls from the refrigerator. Dip about ¾ inch (2 cm) of the end of a 6-inch (15 cm)-long candy stick into the melted lavender candy melts. While still hot, insert this end into the center of a cake ball and use your hand to secure and position the ball securely on the stick.

Dip the cake ball (now secured to the candy stick) back into the melted candy melts and lightly twist the stick in a counterclockwise motion until the entire ball is completely covered.

While the frosting is still wet, sprinkle dried lavender on top of the cake pop. Place the frosted and decorated cake pop into a Styrofoam brick or cake pop rack to let cool and dry. Repeat the above steps for all twenty-four cake pops.

Red Velvet

Red velvet is the little red dress of the baking world. It's always visually stunning, whether you're talking about cake, cupcakes or in this case, cake pops. It's also velvety-soft in texture and coats your taste buds ever so sweetly. The apple cider vinegar really plays up the sweetness (even more so than white vinegar), leaving you with perfectly rich, moist and flavor-dense goodness. These cake pops look wonderful in a bouquet . . . something to consider for Valentine's Day or your upcoming anniversary.

YIELD 2 DOZEN CAKE POPS

RED VELVET CAKE

2 ½ C (248 g) cake flour, sifted

2 tbsp (14 g) unsweetened cocoa powder

1 tsp salt

1 ½ tbsp (22 ml) red food coloring

1 C (236 ml) buttermilk

1 C (236 ml) vegetable oil

1 ½ C (287 g) granulated sugar

2 large eggs

1 tsp vanilla extract

1 ½ tsp baking soda

1 tsp apple cider vinegar

CREAM CHEESE FROSTING

Makes about 3 ⅔ cups (457 g) frosting

(1) 8 oz (226 g) package cream cheese, softened

¼ C (57 g) butter, at room temperature

1 ½ tsp (7.4 ml) vanilla extract

2 C (260 g) confectioners' sugar, plus more if needed

1 (12 oz [340 g]) bag red candy melts

1 (3 oz [85 g]) bottle white nonpareils, for garnish

Preheat the oven to 350°F (176°C). Grease and flour a 9 x 13-inch (22 x 33 cm) baking pan.

To prepare the cake: In a medium bowl, sift the cake flour. Add the cocoa powder and salt and mix together with a whisk. In a liquid measuring cup, stir the buttermilk and red food coloring together; set aside.

In a large bowl, cream together the oil, granulated sugar, eggs and vanilla with an electric mixer at high speed until well combined. Alternate adding the flour mixture and buttermilk a third at a time to the wet ingredients, beating well after each addition until all combined together.

In a small bowl, stir the baking soda and the apple cider vinegar together (will bubble slightly) and incorporate into the batter, stirring gently with a spatula until combined.

Pour the batter into the prepared cake pan and bake for 30 to 35 minutes (if necessary, cover the top with foil toward the end of baking so the top does not brown). Remove from the oven and let cool until no longer warm to the touch.

To prepare the frosting: In a large bowl, beat the cream cheese, butter and vanilla together with an electric mixer on high speed until smooth and fluffy. Add the confectioners' sugar in two additions. Beat until creamy, adding more sugar, if needed, for a slightly thick consistency.

To prepare the candy melts: Place half of the bag of red candy melts in an electric melter, stirring occasionally until smooth. Add the remaining half of the bag and stir until smooth. Turn the melter setting to low and stir occasionally until the candy melts are ready to use. Alternatively, if you don't have an electric melter, you can use your microwave set at 50 percent to melt the candy. In a microwave-safe bowl, heat in increments of 15 seconds, stirring between each heating until melted.

(continued)

To assemble the cake pops: In a large bowl, break apart the entire cake in sections until you get fine crumbles (should resemble bread crumbs). Add the cream cheese frosting 1 to 2 tablespoons (14 to 28 g) at a time, blending well with a spatula after each addition. You will start to see "dough" forming. Stop adding the frosting once the cake dough is the consistency of Play-Doh: moist but not soggy. Start molding the dough into a large bowl with your hands, picking out any dry pieces of cake as you form. Cover with plastic wrap or aluminum foil and chill the dough for 1 to 2 hours, until firm.

Remove the large cake ball from the refrigerator. Taking a small handful of dough with your fingertips, form a small cake ball about 2 inches (5 cm) in diameter (a little smaller than a golf ball) and roll between your hands until smooth and even. Repeat until you get twenty-four cake balls all equal in size. Pile into a large bowl, cover and chill for 20 to 30 minutes, until firm to the touch.

Remove your cake balls from the refrigerator. Dip about ¾ inch (2 cm) of the end of a 6-inch (15 cm)-long candy stick into the melted red candy melts. While still hot, insert this end into the center of a cake ball and use your hand to secure and position the ball securely on the stick.

Dip the cake ball (now secured to the candy stick) back into the melted candy melts and lightly twist the stick in a counterclockwise motion until the entire ball is completely covered.

While the frosting is still wet, sprinkle white nonpareils on all sides of the cake pop. Place the frosted and decorated cake pop into a Styrofoam brick or cake pop rack to let cool and dry. Repeat the above steps for all twenty-four cake pops.

Pancakes & Bacon

As you may have guessed just by looking at some of the titles of my recipes throughout this cookbook, I *love* breakfast! I basically use any excuse to create a sweet treat that I can enjoy at the start of my day, as well as for a party or event. I loved pancakes so much as a kid, I would have my mom make a couple extra—just so I could eat them cold throughout the rest of the day. As for the bacon, well, it's optional, but who doesn't love bacon and pancakes? Breakfast on a stick never looked so cute!

YIELD: 2 DOZEN CAKE POPS

MAPLE SYRUP CAKE

4 C (359 g) cake flour

4 tsp (15 g) baking powder

½ tsp salt

¾ C (172 g) butter, at room temperature

¾ C (143 g) granulated sugar

3 large eggs

1 ½ C (354 ml) pure maple syrup

¾ C (177 ml) buttermilk

1 tsp vanilla extract

½ tsp ground ginger

MAPLE BUTTER FROSTING

Makes about 3 ⅔ cups (457 g) frosting

¼ C (57 g) butter, at room temperature

¼ C (48 g) pure maple syrup

1 tsp vanilla extract

2 C (260 g) confectioners' sugar, plus more if needed

1 (12 oz [340 g]) bag white candy melts

1 lb (453 g) bacon, fried and crumbled, for garnish

Preheat the oven to 350°F (176°C). Grease and flour a 9 x 13-inch (22 x 33 cm) baking pan.

To prepare the cake: Sift the cake flour, baking powder and salt two or three times into a medium-size bowl; set aside.

In a large mixing bowl, cream the butter thoroughly using an electric mixer at high speed, adding the granulated sugar gradually; continue creaming until light and fluffy. Add the eggs, one at a time, beating well after each addition.

In a liquid measuring cup, add the maple syrup to the buttermilk. Alternately add the flour mixture and the buttermilk mixture to the butter mixture; mix well. Add the vanilla and ginger; stir until just combined.

Pour the batter into the prepared cake pan and bake for 30 to 35 minutes (cover the top with foil toward the end of baking so the top does not brown). Remove from the oven and let cool until no longer warm to the touch.

To prepare the frosting: In a large bowl, beat the butter using an electic mixer at medium speed, adding the maple syrup and vanilla, until smooth. Add the confectioners' sugar in two additions. Beat until creamy, adding more sugar, if needed, for a slightly thick consistency.

To prepare the candy melts: Heat half of the white candy melts in an electric melter, stirring occasionally, until smooth. Add the remaining half of the bag and stir until smooth. Turn the melter setting to low and stir the candy melts occasionally until ready to use. Alternatively, if you don't have an electric melter, you can use your microwave set at 50 percent to melt the candy. In a microwave-safe bowl, heat in increments of 15 seconds, stirring between each heating until melted.

(continued)

To assemble the cake pops: In a large bowl, break apart the entire cake in sections until you get fine crumbles (should resemble bread crumbs). Add the maple butter frosting 1 to 2 tablespoons (14 to 28 g) at a time, blending well with a spatula after each addition. You will start to see "dough" forming. Stop adding the frosting once the cake dough is the consistency of Play-Doh: moist but not soggy. Start molding the dough into a large bowl with your hands, picking out any dry pieces of cake as you form. Cover and chill the dough for 1 to 2 hours, until firm.

Remove the large cake ball from the refrigerator. Taking a small handful of dough with your fingertips, form a small cake ball about 2 inches (5 cm) in diameter (a little smaller than a golf ball) and roll between your hands until smooth and even. Repeat until you get twenty- four cake balls all equal in size. Pile into a large bowl, cover and chill for 20 to 30 minutes, until firm to the touch.

Remove your cake balls from the refrigerator. Dip about ¾ inch (2 cm) of the end of a 6-inch (15 cm)-long candy stick into the melted white candy melts. While still hot, insert this end into the center of a cake ball and use your hand to secure and position the ball securely on the stick.

Dip the cake ball (now secured to the candy stick) back into the melted candy melts and lightly twist the stick in a counterclockwise motion until the entire ball is completely covered.

While the frosting is still wet, sprinkle crumbled bacon pieces on top of the cake pop. Place the frosted and decorated cake pop into a Styrofoam brick or cake pop rack to let cool and dry. Repeat the above steps for all twenty-four cake pops.

Peppermint Cocoa

I love adding a little bit of peppermint to my hot cocoa in the winter; that was my inspiration for this little holiday pop. Although not served hot, the cake boasts a dense and rich chocolate flavor that is definitely warming (to your soul) while you enjoy it. The creamy white chocolate melts in your mouth and the beautiful red-and-white striped candy leaves a wintery-fresh finish. These look wonderful as a holiday centerpiece, or individually wrapped and boxed for a simple and delicious gift.

YIELD 2 DOZEN CAKE POPS

CHOCOLATE CAKE

2 C (383 g) granulated sugar

1 ¾ C (335 g) all-purpose flour

¾ C (83 g) unsweetened cocoa powder

1 ½ tsp (6.1 g) baking soda

1 ½ tsp (5.3 g) baking powder

1 tsp salt

2 large eggs

1 C (236 ml) milk

½ C (118 ml) vegetable oil

2 tsp (10 ml) vanilla extract

1 C (236 ml) boiling water

CREAMY CHOCOLATE FROSTING
Makes about 3 ⅔ cups (457 g) frosting

2 ¾ C (357 g) confectioners' sugar

6 tbsp (41 g) unsweetened cocoa powder

6 tbsp (86 g) butter, at room temperature

5 tbsp (74 ml) evaporated milk

1 tsp vanilla extract

1 (12 oz [340 g]) bag white candy melts

12 oz (340 g) crushed hard peppermint candies, for garnish

Preheat the oven to 350°F (176°C). Grease and flour a 9 x 13-inch (22 x 33 cm) baking pan.

To prepare the cake: In a medium-size bowl, stir together granulated sugar, flour, cocoa, baking soda, baking powder and salt. Add the eggs, milk, oil and vanilla; beat with an electric mixer for 3 minutes. Stir in the boiling water by hand.

Pour into the prepared baking pan and bake for 35 to 40 minutes, or until a toothpick inserted into the center comes out clean. Let cool until no longer warm to the touch.

To prepare the frosting: In a medium-size bowl, sift together the confectioners' sugar and cocoa powder; set aside. In a large bowl, cream the butter until smooth, then alternately beat the cocoa mixture and the evaporated milk into the butter. Blend in the vanilla. Beat until light and fluffy, adding more sugar or milk as needed to thicken or thin.

To prepare the candy melts: Heat half of the white candy melts in an electric melter, stirring occasionally, until smooth. Add the remaining half of the bag and stir until smooth. Turn the melter setting to low, and stir the candy melts occasionally until ready to use. Alternatively, if you don't have an electric melter, you can use your microwave set at 50 percent to melt the candy. In a microwave-safe bowl, heat in increments of 15 seconds, stirring between each heating until melted.

(continued)

To assemble the cake pops: In a large bowl, break apart the entire cake in sections until you get fine crumbles (should resemble bread crumbs). Add the chocolate frosting 1 to 2 tablespoons (14 to 28 g) at a time, blending well with a spatula after each addition. You will start to see "dough" forming. Stop adding the frosting once the cake dough is the consistency of Play-Doh: moist but not soggy. Start molding the dough into a large bowl with your hands, picking out any dry pieces of cake as you form. Chill the dough for 1 to 2 hours, until firm.

Remove the large cake ball from the refrigerator. Taking a small handful of dough with your fingertips, form a small cake ball about 2 inches (5 cm) in diameter (a little smaller than a golf ball) and roll between your hands until smooth and even. Repeat until you get twenty-four cake balls all equal in size. Pile into a large bowl, cover and chill for 20 to 30 minutes, until firm to the touch.

Remove your cake balls from the refrigerator. Dip about ¾ inch (2 cm) of the end of a 6-inch (15-cm)-long candy stick into the melted white candy melts. While still hot, insert this end into the center of a cake ball and use your hand to secure and position the ball securely on the stick.

Dip the cake ball (now secured to the candy stick) back into the melted candy melts and lightly twist the stick in a counterclockwise motion until the entire ball is completely covered.

While the frosting is still wet, sprinkle peppermint candy pieces on top of the cake pop. Place the frosted and decorated cake pop into a Styrofoam brick or cake pop rack to let cool and dry. Repeat the above steps for all twenty-four cake pops.

Tangerine Cheesecake

Although you may substitute common-variety orange in lieu of tangerines for this recipe, I do encourage you to search for tangerines and use them if they aren't too hard to find. The subtle differences between these two citrus fruits are slight but important when wanting to use a specific flavor profile in your baking. The tangerine is smaller in size than the orange, so I find it is more concentrated when juicing. It is also less acidic and less tart, which is what I wanted for this delectable cheesecake pop.

YIELD 2 DOZEN CAKE POPS

CITRUS CAKE

2 ¾ C (247 g) cake flour

1 ⅔ C (319 g) granulated sugar

1 tbsp (3 g) baking powder

¾ tsp salt

¾ C (172 g) unsalted butter, at room temperature

4 large eggs

1 C (236 ml) whole milk

1 ¼ C (295 ml) freshly squeezed tangerine juice

2 tsp vanilla extract

Tangerine zest

1 (4 oz [113 g]) package cheesecake instant pudding and pie mix

CREAM CHEESE FROSTING

Makes about 3 ⅔ cups (457 g) frosting

1 (8 oz [226 g]) package cream cheese, softened

¼ C (57 g) butter, at room temperature

1 ½ tsp (7.4 ml) vanilla extract

2 C (260 g) confectioners' sugar, plus more if needed

½ (12 oz [340 g]) bag white candy melts

½ (12 oz [340 g]) bag orange candy melts

16 oz (453 g) graham crackers, crumbled, for garnish

Preheat the oven to 350°F (176°C). Grease and flour a 9 x 13-inch (22 x 33 cm) baking pan.

To prepare the cake: In a medium bowl, sift the cake flour, then add the granulated sugar, baking powder, salt and instant cheesecake pudding/pie mix and whisk together well.

In a large bowl, cream the butter and eggs with an electric mixer at medium speed until smooth, then alternatively beat the flour mixture, the milk and the tangerine juice into the butter mixture. Blend in the vanilla and tangerine zest.

Pour into the prepared baking pan and bake for 35 to 40 minutes, or until a toothpick inserted into the center comes out clean. Remove from the oven and let cool until no longer warm to the touch.

To prepare the frosting: In a large bowl, beat the cream cheese, butter and vanilla together until smooth and fluffy. Add the confectioners' sugar in two additions. Beat until creamy, adding more sugar, if needed, for a slightly thick consistency.

(continued)

To prepare the candy melts: Heat the half-bag of white candy melts in an electric melter, stirring occasionally, until smooth. Add the half-bag of orange candy melts to the melted white candy and stir until smooth (should turn a light orange color). Turn the melter setting to low and stir the candy melts occasionally until ready to use. Alternatively, if you don't have an electric melter, you can use your microwave set at 50 percent to melt the candy. In a microwave-safe bowl, heat in increments of 15 seconds, stirring between each heating until melted.

To assemble the cake pops: In a large bowl, break apart the entire cake in sections until you get fine crumbles (should resemble bread crumbs). Add the cream cheese frosting 1 to 2 tablespoons (14 to 28 g) at a time, blending well with a spatula after each addition. You will start to see "dough" forming. Stop adding the frosting once the cake dough is the consistency of Play-Doh: moist but not soggy. Start molding the dough into a large bowl with your hands, picking out any dry pieces of cake as you form. Chill the dough for 1 to 2 hours, until firm.

Remove the large cake ball from the refrigerator. Taking a small handful of dough with your fingertips, form a small cake ball about 2 inches (5 cm) in diameter (a little smaller than a golf ball) and roll between your hands until smooth and even. Repeat until you get twenty-four cake balls all equal in size. Pile into a large bowl, cover and chill for 20 to 30 minutes, until firm to the touch.

Remove your cake balls from the refrigerator. Dip ¾ inch (2 cm) of the end of a 6-inch (15 cm)-long candy stick into the melted candy melt mixture. While still hot, insert this end into the center of a cake ball and use your hand to secure and position the ball securely on the stick.

Dip the cake ball (now secured to the candy stick) back into the melted candy melt mixture and lightly twist the stick in a counterclockwise motion until the entire ball is completely covered.

While the frosting is still wet, sprinkle crumbled graham crackers on top of the cake pop. Place the frosted and decorated cake pop into a Styrofoam brick or cake pop rack to cool and dry. Repeat the above steps for all twenty-four cake pops.

Pumpkin Nut

This recipe was one passed down from my great-grandmother Clara on my mom's side, and my mother and I never changed a thing. She would even bake them in one-pound metal coffee cans, which provided a cylindrical loaf with ring indentures left behind from the can's design (perfect for slicing identical pieces each time). True, this is more of a bread base than a cake, but it works just the same, and delivers a wonderfully dense and nutty cake pop. I've made pumpkin bread, cookies and cupcakes, and these cake pops are far and away my favorite to make and to bring to parties when the occasion calls for something pumpkin!

YIELD: 2 DOZEN CAKE POPS

PUMPKIN NUT CAKE

½ C (114 g) butter, at room temperature

1 ½ C (287 g) granulated sugar

2 large eggs

2 C (198 g) all-purpose flour

1 tsp baking soda

1 tsp salt

½ tsp ground cinnamon

½ tsp ground nutmeg

⅓ C (78 ml) water

1 C (180 g) canned pure pumpkin puree

1 C (120 g) chopped pecans

CREAM CHEESE FROSTING

Makes about 3 ⅔ cups (457 g) frosting

1 8 oz [226 g]) package cream cheese, softened

¼ C (57 g) butter, at room temperature

1 ½ tsp (7.4 g) vanilla extract

2 C (260 g) confectioners' sugar, plus more if needed

1 (12 oz [340 g]) bag white candy melts

12 oz (362 g) finely chopped pecans, for garnish

Preheat the oven to 350°F (176°C). Grease and flour a 9 x 13-inch (22 x 33 cm) baking pan.

To prepare the cake: In a large bowl, cream together the butter and granulated sugar with an electric mixer. Add the eggs, one at a time, beating well after each addition.

In a medium-size bowl, whisk together the flour, baking soda, salt and spices. Alternately add the flour mixture and the water to the butter mixture, starting and ending with the flour mixture. Add the pumpkin and fold in the pecans.

Pour into the prepared baking pan and bake for 30 to 35 minutes, or until a toothpick inserted into the center comes out clean. Remove from the oven and let cool until no longer warm to the touch.

To prepare the frosting: In a large bowl, beat the cream cheese, butter and vanilla together until smooth and fluffy. Add the confectioners' sugar in two additions. Beat until creamy, adding more sugar, if needed, for a slightly thick consistency.

To prepare the candy melts: Heat half of the white candy melts in an electric melter, stirring occasionally, until smooth. Add the remaining half of the bag and stir until smooth. Turn the melter setting to low and stir the candy melts occasionally until ready to use. Alternatively, if you don't have an electric melter, you can use your microwave set at 50 percent to melt the candy. In a microwave-safe bowl, heat in increments of 15 seconds, stirring between each heating until melted.

(continued)

To assemble cake pops: In a large bowl, break apart the entire cake in sections until you get fine crumbles (should resemble bread crumbs). Add the cream cheese frosting 1 to 2 tablespoons (14 to 28 g) at a time, blending well with a spatula after each addition. You will start to see "dough" forming. Stop adding the frosting once the cake dough is the consistency of Play-Doh: moist but not soggy. Start molding the dough into a large bowl with your hands, picking out any dry pieces of cake as you form. Chill the dough for 1 to 2 hours until firm.

Remove the large cake ball from the refrigerator. Taking a small handful of dough with your fingertips, form a small cake ball about 2 inches (5 cm) in diameter (a little smaller than a golf ball) and roll between your hands until smooth and even. Repeat until you get twenty-four cake balls all equal in size. Pile into a large bowl, cover and chill for 20 to 30 minutes, until firm to the touch.

Remove your cake balls from the refrigerator. Dip about ¾ inch (2 cm) of the end of a 6-inch (15 cm)-long candy stick into the melted white candy melts. While still hot, insert this end into the center of a cake ball and use your hand to secure and position the ball securely on the stick.

Dip the cake ball (now secured to the candy stick) back into the melted candy melts and lightly twist the stick in a counterclockwise motion until the entire ball is completely covered.

While the frosting is still wet, sprinkle chopped pecans on all sides of the cake pop. Place the frosted and decorated cake pop into a Styrofoam brick or cake pop rack to cool and dry. Repeat the above steps for all twenty-four cake pops.

Triple Chocolate

Chocolate. Chocolate. Chocolate. You can never have enough. If you're an avid chocoholic, you're going to love this little pop featuring your favorite trio. The key to this decadent chocolate recipe is to use boiling water. It really allows the cocoa to bloom before baking. The pops are then dipped in milk chocolate candy melts (you may also opt for plain milk chocolate) and, finally, garnished with chocolate sprinkles. They look good, they taste good, and they are a crowd-pleasing sure bet!

YIELD: 2 DOZEN CAKE POPS

CHOCOLATE CAKE

2 C (383 g) granulated sugar

1 ¾ C (174 g) all-purpose flour

¾ C (83 g) unsweetened cocoa powder

1 ½ tsp (6.1 g) baking soda

1 ½ tsp (5.3 g) baking powder

1 tsp salt

2 large eggs

1 C (236 ml) milk

½ C (118 ml) vegetable oil

2 tsp (10 ml) vanilla extract

1 C (236 ml) boiling water

CREAMY CHOCOLATE FROSTING

Makes about 3 ⅔ cups (457 g) frosting

2 ¾ C (357 g) confectioners' sugar

6 tbsp (41 g) unsweetened cocoa powder

6 tbsp (86 g) butter, at room temperature

5 tbsp (74 ml) evaporated milk

1 tsp vanilla extract

1 (12 oz [340 g]) bag milk chocolate candy melts

Chocolate sprinkles, for garnish

Preheat the oven to 350°F (176°C). Grease and flour a 9 x 13-inch (22 x 33 cm) baking pan.

To prepare the cake: In a medium-size bowl, stir together granulated sugar, flour, cocoa, baking soda, baking powder and salt. Add the eggs, milk, oil and vanilla; beat with an electric mixer for 3 minutes. Stir in the boiling water by hand.

Pour into the prepared baking pan and bake for 35 to 40 minutes, or until toothpick inserted into the center comes out clean. Remove from the oven and let cool until no longer warm to the touch.

To prepare the frosting: In a medium-size bowl, sift together the confectioners' sugar and cocoa powder; set aside. In a large bowl, cream the butter until smooth, then alternately beat the sugar mixture and the evaporated milk into the butter mixture. Blend in the vanilla. Beat until light and fluffy, adding more sugar or milk as needed to thicken or thin.

To prepare the candy melts: Place half of the milk chocolate candy melts in an electric melter, stirring occasionally, until smooth. Add the remaining half of the bag and stir until smooth. Turn the melter setting to low and stir the candy melts occasionally until ready to use. Alternatively, if you don't have an electric melter, you can use your microwave set at 50 percent to melt the candy. In a microwave-safe bowl, heat in increments of 15 seconds, stirring between each heating until melted.

(continued)

To assemble the cake pops: In a large bowl, break apart the entire cake in sections until you get fine crumbles (should resemble bread crumbs). Add the chocolate frosting 1 to 2 tablespoons (14 to 28 g) at a time, blending well with a spatula after each addition. You will start to see "dough" forming. Stop adding the frosting the cake dough is the consistency of Play-Doh: moist but not soggy. Start molding the dough into a large bowl with your hands, picking out any dry pieces of cake as you form. Chill the dough for 1 to 2 hours, until firm.

Remove the large cake ball from the refrigerator. Taking a small handful of dough with your fingertips, form a small cake ball about 2 inches (5 cm) in diameter (a little smaller than a golf ball) and roll between your hands until smooth and even. Repeat until you get twenty-four cake balls all equal in size. Pile into a large bowl, cover and chill for 20 to 30 minutes, until firm to the touch.

Remove your cake balls from the refrigerator. Dip about ¾ inch (2 cm) of the end of a 6-inch (15 cm)-long candy stick into the melted chocolate candy melts. While still hot, insert this end into the center of a cake ball and use your hand to secure and position the ball securely onto the stick.

Dip the cake ball (now secured to the candy stick) back into the melted candy melts and lightly twist the stick in a counterclockwise motion until the entire ball is completely covered.

While the frosting is still wet, sprinkle chocolate sprinkles on all sides of the cake pop. Place the frosted and decorated cake pop into a Styrofoam brick or cake pop rack to cool and dry. Repeat the above steps for all twenty-four cake pops.

5

Tea Time Mini Loaves

Tea time! I adore tea-themed brunches or simple tea parties; I think it's ingrained from childhood. Scones, finger sandwiches, fruit and cream . . . the food is always so dainty and pretty, it's almost hard to eat it . . . almost.

Everything about mini loaves exudes Cakewalk Desserts. They are small in size, beautiful and delicious, and the different flavor combinations fit into various themed teas parties.

These tiny sweet cakes are baked in mini loaf pans so that they can be cut into slices and be enjoyed with spreads. They are also small enough to enjoy as an entire loaf all at once, much like a muffin or roll. They make for a darling display at each place setting or stacked on a beautiful tiered platter. I've included sweet and savory recipes so there is something for every taste!

TIPS

• Mini loaves will stay fresh for three to five days once they are baked, so if you are making a large quantity, keep this shelf life in mind.

• If the recipe includes fruit, I would recommend refrigerating them if they will be kept for more than twenty-four hours; otherwise, room temperature will be sufficient.

Lemon-Thyme

Citrus and garden herbs are an exquisite pairing. They offer a very organic and refreshing twist to the palate. This mini loaf pairs well with almost any kind of white, herbal or black tea, and is a fail-safe plan if you are only going to provide one option for your hosted event. I make these loaves wrapped with twine and topped with a sprig of fresh thyme. It is simple but thoughtful and a huge hit. Never underestimate the homemade touch.

YIELDS: 8 MINI LOAVES OR ONE 9″ X 5″ (22 X 12 CM) LOAF

½ C (114 g) butter, at room temperature

¾ C (143 g) sugar

1 large egg

1 tsp vanilla extract

1 ¾ C (174 g) all-purpose flour

½ tsp baking soda

¼ tsp salt

2 tbsp (4 g) fresh thyme, minced

2 tbsp (11 g) lemon zest

½ C (118 ml) buttermilk

½ C (118 ml) sour cream

Fresh thyme sprigs, for garnish

Preheat the oven to 350°F (176°C). Grease and flour an eight-loaf linked mini loaf pan or one 9 x 5-inch (22 x 12 cm) loaf pan.

In a large mixing bowl, cream the butter and sugar with an electric mixer until light and fluffy. Beat in the egg and vanilla and continue mixing for 1 minute.

In another bowl, whisk together the flour, baking soda, salt, thyme and lemon zest.

In a liquid measuring cup, measure out the buttermilk and add the sour cream, stirring until combined. Alternately add the buttermilk mixture and the flour mixture to the butter mixture, beating well after each addition.

Transfer to the prepared mini loaf pan and bake for 15 to 20 minutes (or 25 to 35 minutes using a 9 x 5-inch pan [22 x 12 cm]), or until a toothpick inserted into the center comes out clean.

Let cool for at least 15 minutes in the pan before transferring to a cooling rack. Garnish with fresh thyme sprigs secured with twine, for an added touch.

Rocky Road

My husband loves ice cream! I would say it is his favorite sweet indulgence. Since we limit the presence of processed foods in our house, we bought an ice-cream maker and have experimented with all sorts of flavors including yogurts and sorbets. One of our most beloved is Rocky Road. This was the inspiration behind this little mini loaf. It has just the right amount of chocolate, fluff and crunch to include everything you love about the popular iced treat, but in a convenient little loaf! This version you can even enjoy on a cold winter day.

YIELD: 8 MINI LOAVES OR ONE 9″ X 5″ (22 X 12 CM) LOAF

¼ C (30 g) almonds

2 C (298 g) all-purpose flour

2 tsp (7 g) baking powder

2 tbsp (24 g) sugar

½ tsp salt

¼ C (57 g) butter

1 C (50 g) mini marshmallows

¾ C (177 g) milk

1 large egg, lightly beaten

1 C (180 g) chocolate chips

Preheat the oven to 350°F (176°C). Grease and flour an eight-loaf linked mini loaf pan or one 9 x 5-inch (22 x 12 cm) loaf pan.

To toast the almonds: Spread out the almonds in one layer on an ungreased, shallow baking pan. Bake for 10 to 15 minutes, stirring occasionally until golden. Once they are cool to the touch, you can chop the almonds coarsely.

To prepare the cakes: Mix the flour, baking powder, sugar and salt together in a large bowl and cut in the butter until the mixture resembles coarse bread crumbs. Stir in the marshmallows and toasted almonds, mixing well.

In a separate bowl, combine milk and egg; pour into the flour mixture and stir just to moisten. Fold in the chocolate chips.

Transfer to the prepared mini loaf pan and bake for 15 to 20 minutes (or 25 to 35 minutes using a 9 x 5-inch pan [22 x 12 cm]), or until a toothpick inserted into the center comes out clean.

Let cool for at least 15 minutes in the pan before transferring to a cooling rack and serving.

Kalamata Olive & Oregano

Greek salad is a great way to spice up your routine lunch, or in this case makes a wonderful savory mini loaf. It was an easy choice, as I'm a big salt junkie and always a fan of olives! The fresh oregano balances the butter and salt in this recipe and I think the name alone will get people interested. This savory loaf pairs particularly well with a Darjeeling black tea. *Opa!*

YIELD: 8 MINI LOAVES OR ONE 9″ X 5″ (22 X 12 CM) LOAF

1 tbsp (14 ml) olive oil

1 C (151 g) finely chopped yellow onion

2 C (198 g) all-purpose flour

1 tsp baking soda

½ tsp salt

1 C (236 ml) buttermilk

2 tbsp (28 g) butter, melted

2 large eggs

1 C (180 g) pitted and chopped kalamata olives

3 tbsp (9 g) fresh oregano, chopped plus extra for sprinkling on loaves

Preheat the oven to 350°F (176°C). Grease and flour an eight-loaf linked mini loaf pan or one 9 x 5-inch (22 x 12 cm) loaf pan.

Heat the oil in a large, nonstick skillet over medium heat; add the onion and sauté for 3 minutes, or until tender. Set aside.

Combine the flour, baking soda and salt in a large bowl and make a well in the center of the mixture.

In a separate bowl, combine the buttermilk, melted butter and eggs, stirring with a whisk. Pour the buttermilk mixture into the well of the flour mixture, stirring just until moistened. Fold in the cooked onions, olives and oregano.

Transfer to the prepared mini loaf pan and sprinkle the tops with more chopped oregano. Bake for 15 to 20 minutes (or 25 to 35 minutes using a 9 x 5-inch pan [22 x 12 cm]), or until a toothpick inserted into the center comes out clean.

Let cool for at least 15 minutes in the pan before transferring to a cooling rack and serving.

Orange Blueberry

This mini loaf is wonderfully moist, a little tangy and smells so good while baking, it's almost therapeutic. Blueberries are a great fruit to share the stage with it, as they have just the right amount of sweetness, sourness and juiciness. Lemon is a common pairing, but I found that oranges add that subtle tang without overdoing the tartness. One taste of these babies and you'll think twice before making plain ole blueberry muffins again.

YIELD: 8 MINI LOAVES OR ONE 9″ X 5″ (22 X 12 CM) LOAF

2 ¼ C (223 g) all-purpose flour

1 tbsp (15 g) baking powder

1 tsp salt

¼ C (57 g) butter, at room temperature

¾ C (150 g) brown sugar, firmly packed

1 large egg

½ C (118 ml) buttermilk

¼ C (59 ml) freshly squeezed orange juice

2 tbsp (11 g) orange zest

1 C (99 g) fresh blueberries

Preheat the oven to 350°F (176°C). Grease and flour an eight-loaf linked mini loaf pan or one 9 x 5-inch (22 x 12 cm) loaf pan.

In a medium-size mixing bowl, whisk together the flour, baking powder and salt.

In a large bowl, cream together the butter and brown sugar with an electric mixer on medium speed. Add the egg, buttermilk, orange juice and orange zest, beating well after each addition.

Add the flour mixture to the sugar mixture. Mix at low speed until well blended, then beat at medium speed for 2 minutes. Fold in the blueberries.

Transfer to the prepared mini loaf pan and bake for 20 to 25 minutes (or 25 to 35 minutes using a 9 x 5-inch pan [22 x 12 cm]), or until a toothpick inserted into the center comes out clean.

Let cool for at least 15 minutes in the pan before transferring to a cooling rack and let cool for an additional 10 to 15 minutes before serving.

Nonna's Zucchini

My mother, who is now Nonna (Italian for "grandma") was my first teacher and mentor in the kitchen. While I was growing up, she always kept a big garden full of vegetables and would even use them in her baking. Zucchini bread has always been a favorite way to eat green among my siblings and me, even when we were too young to realize Mom was being sneaky about getting us to eat our vegetables. The zucchini gives this mini loaf a rich denseness that complements the nuts and cinnamon. Aesthetically, it also gives the loaf a beautiful harvest green color that really pops on the plate.

YIELD: 8 MINI LOAVES OR ONE 9″ X 5″ (22 X 12 CM) LOAF

3 C (298 g) all-purpose flour

1 tsp salt

1 tsp baking powder

1 tsp baking soda

1 tbsp (8 g) ground cinnamon

3 large eggs

1 C (236 ml) vegetable oil

1 tbsp (14 ml) vanilla extract

2 ¼ C (431 g) sugar

2 C (151 g) grated zucchini (skin on)

1 C (116 g) chopped walnuts

Preheat the oven to 325°F (162°C). Grease and flour an eight-loaf linked mini loaf pan or one 9 x 5-inch (22 x 12 cm) loaf pan.

Sift together the flour, salt, baking powder, baking soda and cinnamon in a bowl. Beat the eggs, oil, vanilla and sugar together in a large bowl.

Add the dry ingredients to the wet mixture and beat well. Stir in the zucchini and nuts until well combined (be careful not to overstir).

Pour the batter three-quarters of the way full into each mini loaf pan and bake for 15 to 20 minutes (or 25 to 35 minutes using a 9 x 5-inch pan [22 x 12 cm]), or until a toothpick inserted into the center comes out clean.

Let cool for at least 15 minutes in the pan before transferring to a cooling rack and serving.

Peanut Butter Banana

One of my all-time favorite things to eat while I was pregnant with my son, Quintus, was toast with peanut butter and sliced bananas on top. The craving was so intense, I ate it almost every day, and even now I still enjoy it maybe one or two times per week. It was definitely the inspiration for this mini loaf, and it's great because I can always bake it over the weekend and enjoy throughout the week without the fuss! It's loaded with good stuff, so while it is a sweet treat, it's one that you can munch with limited guilt.

YIELD: 8 MINI LOAVES OR ONE 9″ X 5″ (22 X 12 CM) LOAF

---

3 overripe bananas, mashed

⅓ C (40 g) plain yogurt

1 C (180 g) crunchy peanut butter (natural is best)

3 tbsp (43 g) butter, melted

2 large eggs

½ C (95 g) granulated sugar

½ C (100 g) brown sugar, packed

1 tsp vanilla extract

1 ½ C (149 g) all-purpose flour

¾ tsp baking soda

½ tsp salt

½ tsp ground cinnamon

⅛ tsp ground allspice

Preheat the oven to 350°F (176°C). Grease and flour an eight-loaf linked mini loaf pan or one 9 x 5-inch (22 x 12 cm) loaf pan.

In a large bowl, combine the bananas, yogurt, peanut butter, melted butter and eggs and beat with an electric mixer on medium speed. Add the granulated sugar, brown sugar and vanilla; beat until blended.

In a separate bowl, combine the flour, baking soda, salt, cinnamon and allspice. Add the flour mixture to the banana mixture; beat until just blended.

Pour the batter three-quarters of the way full into each mini loaf pan and bake for 20 to 25 minutes (or 25 to 35 minutes using a 9 x 5-inch pan [22 x 12 cm]), or until a toothpick tester inserted into the center comes out clean.

Let cool for at least 15 minutes in the pan before transferring to a cooling rack and serving.

Butter, Beer & Cheese

This savory little brew cake is sure to be a clear favorite in the male arena—so much so,
that you may find it works as well for Monday night football as it does for your next tea or brunch.
The butter and cheese are extra creamy and perfectly seasoned with the garlic and onion.
You can use any lager-style beer, which is best for this application because of its subtle
bitterness and hop levels. It's another great pairing with any black tea.

YIELD: 8 MINI LOAVES OR ONE 9" X 5" (22 X 12 CM) LOAF

---

1 tbsp (14 ml) olive oil

½ C (75 g) finely chopped yellow onion,

¼ tsp freshly ground black pepper

1 garlic clove, minced

3 C (298 g) all-purpose flour

3 tbsp (36 g) sugar

2 tsp (7 g) baking powder

1 tsp salt

¼ C (12 g) chopped green onions

½ C (60 g) shredded Monterey Jack cheese

1 C (130 g) shredded sharp cheddar cheese

1 (12 oz [340 ml]) can lager-style beer

6 tbsp (86 g) melted butter

Preheat the oven to 375°F (190°C). Grease and flour an eight-loaf linked mini loaf pan or one 9 x 5-inch (22 x 12 cm) loaf pan.

Heat the oil in a small skillet over medium-low heat. Add the onion to the pan and cook, stirring occasionally, for 10 minutes, or until browned. Stir in the pepper and garlic and cook for 1 minute.

Combine the flour, sugar, baking powder and salt in a large bowl, stirring with a whisk; make a well in the center of the mixture.

In a separate bowl, stir together the onion mixture, green onions, Monterey Jack and cheddar cheese and beer; pour into the well of the flour mixture, stirring until just moistened.

Pour the batter three-quarters of the way full into each mini loaf pan and drizzle half of the melted butter over each mini loaf. Bake for 15 minutes, then pour the remaining melted butter over the mini loaves and bake for an additional 5 to 10 minutes, or until a toothpick inserted into the center comes out clean. If using a 9 x 5-inch (22 x 12 cm) pan, bake for 20 minutes, add the butter, then bake for 20 more minutes.

Let cool for at least 15 minutes in the pan before transferring to a cooling rack. Serve warm with butter.

Walnut Streusel

I never tire of streusel-topped desserts. Not only does streusel add that perfect crunch, but it also helps seal in moisture for a soft and fluffy cake. That is the stuff dreams are made of! Walnuts add a little something extra to the traditional streusel, and although we have walnuts in abundance in California, you can use any nut you'd prefer. This recipe, while simple, is attractive, appetizing and is always a frontrunner.

YIELD: 8 MINI LOAVES OR ONE 9" X 5" (22 X 12 CM) LOAF

STREUSEL

⅓ C (67 g) brown sugar, packed

⅓ C (26 g) old-fashioned rolled oats

1 tbsp (6 g) all-purpose flour

¼ tsp ground cinnamon

Pinch of salt

2 tbsp (28 g) butter, melted

¼ C (29 g) chopped walnuts

CAKE

2 C (198 g) all-purpose flour

½ tsp baking soda

½ tsp baking powder

½ tsp salt

5 tbsp (71 g) butter, at room temperature

⅔ C (127 g) granulated sugar

3 large eggs

1 tsp vanilla extract

1 C (236 ml) buttermilk

Preheat the oven to 350°F (176°C). Grease and flour an eight-loaf linked mini loaf pan or one 9 x 5-inch (22 x 12 cm) loaf pan.

To prepare the streusel: In a mixing bowl, combine the brown sugar, rolled oats, flour, cinnamon and salt. Add the melted butter, stirring until well combined. Stir in the nuts and set aside

To prepare the cakes: Combine the flour, baking soda, baking powder and salt in a mixing bowl, stirring well with a whisk.

In a large mixing bowl, beat the butter and granulated sugar with an electric mixer on medium speed until well blended. Add the eggs, one at a time, beating well after each addition. Beat in the vanilla.

Beating at low speed, alternately add the flour mixture and the buttermilk to the sugar mixture (beginning and ending with the flour mixture); beat until just combined.

Pour the batter three-quarters of the way full into each mini loaf pan and sprinkle the streusel topping on top of each mini loaf. Bake for 20 to 25 minutes (or 25 to 35 minutes using a 9 x 5-inch pan [22 x 12 cm]), or until a toothpick inserted into the center comes out clean.

Let cool for at least 15 minutes in the pan before transferring to a cooling rack and let cool for an additional 10 to 15 minutes before serving.

Raspberry Cream

I find that raspberries eaten alone are best the day you pick (or buy) them. However, I always end up buying more than I can eat in a day. If you find yourself needing to use up some of these yummy little berries, especially if they are past their prime, this quick and easy recipe is perfect! I made these for my sister's tea-themed baby shower, and everyone raved about them. Display them in a clear cellophane bag, add a cute tag and you have a creative and edible favor that's right on theme.

YIELD: 8 MINI LOAVES OR ONE 9" X 5" (22 X 12 CM) LOAF

⅓ C (80 g) cream cheese, softened

⅓ C (76 g) butter, at room temperature

1 ½ C (287 g) sugar

2 large eggs

1 ½ tsp vanilla extract

2 C (198 g) all-purpose flour

1 tsp baking powder

¼ tsp baking soda

½ tsp salt

½ C (121 ml) buttermilk

2 C (198 g) raspberries

¼ C (29 g) chopped macadamia nuts

Preheat the oven to 350°F (176°C). Grease and flour an eight-load linked mini loaf pan or one 9 x 5-inch (22 x 12 cm) loaf pan.

In a large bowl, beat the cream cheese and butter with an electric mixer on high speed until well blended. Add the sugar and beat until fluffy. Add the eggs, one at a time, beating well after each addition. Beat in the vanilla.

Combine the flour, baking powder, baking soda and salt in a separate bowl. With the mixer on low speed, alternately add the flour mixture and the buttermilk to the cream cheese mixture (beginning and ending with the flour mixture). Gently fold in the raspberries and macadamia nuts.

Pour the batter three-quarters of the way full into each mini loaf and bake for 20 to 25 minutes (or 25 to 35 minutes using a 9 x 5-inch pan [22 x 12 cm]), or until a toothpick inserted into the center comes out clean.

Let cool for at least 30 minutes in the pan before transferring to a cooling rack and serving.

Top with fresh raspberries for added color and flavor.

Golden Harvest

"Everything but the kitchen sink" would be another great name for this eclectic little tea bread. It has wonderful flavor, lots of texture and beautiful colors all wrapped up in one little morsel. Raisins add a sweet and chewy addition, but a trip to your local market might inspire you to use another dried fruit, such as cranberries or dates. It's not quite pumpkin bread, not quite carrot cake . . . not quite like anything you've tasted before. It's in a word, delicious!

YIELD: 8 MINI LOAVES OR ONE 9" X 5" (22 X 12 CM) LOAF

BUTTERMILK GLAZE
1 C (191 g) sugar
1 ½ tsp (6 g) baking soda
½ C (118 ml) buttermilk
½ C (114 g) butter
1 tbsp (14 ml) light corn syrup
1 tsp vanilla extract

CAKE
2 C (198 g) all-purpose flour
½ tbsp baking powder
1 tsp baking soda
½ tsp salt
½ tsp ground cinnamon
½ tsp ground nutmeg
¼ tsp ground allspice
1 C (191 g) sugar
2 large eggs
½ C (118 ml) buttermilk
¼ C (59 ml) canola oil
⅓ C (78 ml) water
8 oz (226 g) canned pure pumpkin puree
¼ C (37 g) raisins
¼ C (85 g) grated carrot
½ C (58 g) finely chopped walnuts

Preheat the oven to 350°F (176°C). Grease and flour an eight-loaf linked mini loaf pan or one 9 x 5-inch (22 x 12 cm) loaf pan.

To prepare the glaze: In a large saucepan, combine the sugar, baking soda, buttermilk, butter and corn syrup; stirring constantly, bring to a boil over medium-high heat and boil for 4 to 5 minutes. Remove from the heat and stir in the vanilla.

To assemble the cakes: Combine the flour, baking powder, baking soda, salt, cinnamon, nutmeg and allspice in a bowl, stirring with a whisk.

In a large bowl, beat the sugar, eggs, buttermilk and oil with an electric mixer on high speed until well blended. Add the water and pumpkin, beating on low speed until blended.

Add the flour mixture to the pumpkin mixture, beating at low speed until just combined. Gently fold in the raisins, carrot and walnuts.

Pour the batter three-quarters of the way full into each mini loaf pan. Bake for 15 to 20 minutes (or 25 to 35 minutes using a 9 x 5-inch pan [22 x 12 cm]), or until a toothpick inserted into the center comes out clean.

Let cool for at least 15 minutes in the pan before transferring to a cooling rack and covering each loaf with the glaze. Let cool for an additional 15 to 20 minutes before serving.

Acknowledgments

I would like to give a very big thank-you to my loving family: to my mother and grandmothers, whose legacy lives on through many of these recipes; to my amazing husband, for always encouraging me to go after my dreams; to my son, Quintus, for giving me precious little smiles that give me enormous strength; and to all of my clients who have allowed me to continue doing what I love to do every day!

Others I would like to give thanks to:

Lisa and Bob Griffith (my wonderful in-laws), for offering up their private residence for my cookbook photo shoot. It's a place where we as a family convene weekly to enjoy good food and wine, laughter and lasting memories. I think that love comes through in this book.

Archive Vintage Rentals (www.archiverentals.com), for supplying various props for my photo shoot. These ladies have some of the coolest vintage furniture and kitchenware to rent. I was like a kid in a candy shop, selecting pieces to use, and hope I can utilize their services again soon.

Sean Smetona (my brother-in-law) of Sean Smetona Design (www.seansmetona.com), for designing my Cakewalk Desserts logo and branding for my business. He is also a genuine baby whisperer, and was a lifesaver watching my son while I worked long hours for the shoot.

My dad, Robert Sheldon, my brother Kyle and my sister Katrina Van Der Wal who have given me the confidence to believe in myself while writing this book. You have always been in my corner through all my ups and downs and supported and loved me through all my crazy hare-brained schemes.

Thank you to all of my extended family and friends for all the support and encouragement you've given to me throughout the years with my business and through this exciting endeavor. I love you all more than words can express!

My husband and I have had a lot of ups and downs in our life together, but the three things that always kept us happy at the end of the day were our family, our faith and good food . . . especially something sweet. I hope all my readers cherish these recipes as much as I do.

Suppliers

Wilton Products (electric chocolate melter, candy melts), www.wilton.com

Chicago Metallics (mini loaf pans). www. cmbakeware.com

Little Yellow Bicycle (tags), www.mylyb.com

Pumped on Paper (favor tags), www.etsy.com/shop/pumpedonpaper

Little Pretty Designs (floral paper straws), www.etsy.com/shop/rb1429

King Arthur Flour, www.kingartherflour.com

Williams-Sonoma (lattice pie mold), www.william-sonoma.com

Fox Run (cookie cutters), www.foxunbrands.com

Bahana Splits Boutique (paper straws, baker's twine, paper bags), www.etsy.com/shop/BahanaSplitsBoutique

Save on Crafts (various props), www.save-on-crafts.com

CB2 (dessert plates and milk cartons), www.cb2.com

About the Author

Andrea Smetona is the owner and founder of Cakewalk Desserts (www.cakewalkdesserts.com) in Laguna Niguel, California. She has been making the pie pop famous nationwide with her mouthwatering recipes and signature peek-a-boo designs since 2010. *Easy as Pie Pops* is her first cookbook. She resides in Laguna Niguel, California with her husband, Ian and son, Quintus.

Index